36

BLACK ARROW, BLUE DIAMOND

BLACK ARROW, BLUE DIAMOND

Squadron Leader Brian Mercer, AFC*

Pen & Sword
AVIATION

First published in
Great Britain in 2006
By Pen & Sword Aviation
An imprint of Pen and Sword Books Ltd
47 Church Street
Barnsley
South Yorkshire
S70 2AS
England

ISBN 1 84415 392 4

A CIP record for this book is available from the British Library.

Typeset in the UK by Mac Style, Nafferton, E. Yorkshire.
Printed and bound in the UK by CPI UK.

Pen & Sword Books Ltd incorporates the imprints of Pen & Sword
Aviation, Pen & Sword Maritime, Pen & Sword Military, Wharncliffe
Local History, Pen & Sword Select, Pen & Sword Military Classics and
Leo Cooper.

For a complete list of Pen & Sword titles please contact
Pen & Sword Books Limited
47 Church Street, Barnsley, South Yorkshire, S70 2AS, England
E-mail: enquiries@pen-and-sword.co.uk
Website: www.pen-and-sword.co.uk

Contents

Explanation of Terms and Abbreviations

ADF (Automatic Direction Finder)
A cockpit instrument that gives the bearing to a radio beacon or broadcast station. Also called a Radio Compass.

AOC
Air Officer Commanding

AI (Airborne Interception)
Radar set fitted to night fighters, eg A1 Mark 10, A1 Mark 21.

ASV (Air/Surface Vessel)
Radar set carried by Coastal Command aircraft to search for ships.

AVPIN (ISO-Propyl-Nitrate)
Used in the starting system on some military jet engines. This liquid is squirted into a combustion chamber and ignited. The resulting explosion then spins the engine

Balbo
A large formation named after the Italian General Balbo, famous for leading large formations of aircraft in the 1930s.

Battle Formation
A loose formation used by fighters in a combat area. Amazingly in the 1960s we still used the tactics first developed by the Luftwaffe Condor Legion during the Spanish Civil War. Hard lessons learned during the Battle of Britain caused the RAF to adopt the German system.

Bought The Farm
An american expression meaning to have crashed or met with disaster.

CRDF (Cathode Ray Direction Finder)
An instrument like a TV screen situated in the air traffic control tower which gives an instant bearing to an aircraft transmitting on VHF (very high frequency).

DME (Distance Measuring Equipment)
A cockpit instrument which gives the distance in nautical miles to which ever beacon is tuned in. It had line of sight range and was reasonably reliable.

Dutch Roll
A combination of roll and yaw to which swept-wing aircraft are susceptible, particularly at high altitude. This phenomenon can become uncomfortable or even dangerous if allowed to persist. The corrective action is either to descend to a lower altitude or to apply a sharp aileron input against the rising wing. All modern swept-wing aircraft are fitted with a yaw damper which stops this from happening.

Forward Radar Control Post
Mobile radar station which could tell an aircraft flying at a known height and airspeed, when to release its bombs to hit a target.

Finger Four
Tactical formation flown by four fighters, positioned like the fingertips of an outstretched hand.

GCA (Ground Controlled Approach)
Airfield radar which enables the controller to give radio instructions to a pilot to keep him lined-up with the runway

and on the glideslope. The effectiveness of this aid was dependent on the skill of the controller and the pilot. It was out standard method of recovering fighters in bad weather and its use had proved vital during the Berlin Airlift.

GCI (Ground Controlled Interception)
The air defence radars were called GCI stations.

GEE
A navigation aid developed for Bomber Command during World War Two. Parabolic position line are superimposed on a chart and a navigator could determine his position by interpreting the signals from a master and two slave transmitting stations on a cathode-ray tube installed in the aircraft.

Hap Arnold Scheme
Name given to the scheme for training RAF pilots in the USA before America entered World War Two. Named after the commander of the US Army Air Corps.

ILS (Instrument Landing System)
Airfield radar that transmitted signals to an aircraft on the approach and allowed the pilot to make corrections to his flight path to stay on the glideslope and lined-up with the runway. The information was given to the pilot usually by a flight director instrument and a skilled pilot could follow the flight director commands down to about 100 ft. above the ground. It could be a demanding task on a wet and windy night at Kai Tak airport, Hong Kong, in conditions of bad turbulence and constantly changing drift.

Mach Number
Aircraft speed expressed as a percentage of the speed of sound. For example a Mach number of 0.85 equals eighty five per cent of the speed of sound.

QFI (Qualified Flying Instructor).

SBAC (Society of British Aircraft Constructors).

SSB (Single Side Board)
Efficient type of HF (high frequency) radar for long-range radio communications.

Telescramble
A direct land line from the radar station to the pilot in his cockpit. This line disconnects when the aircraft moves forward. A hunter pilot sitting in his cockpit on the operational readiness platform at the end of the runway with his engine off, could be airbourne sixty seconds after the order to scramble.

VOR (VHF Omni Range)
A radio beacon on very high frequency that gives the pilot a bearing to the beacon. Line-of-sight range and more accurate and reliable than ADF.

Wet Lease
The leasing of an aircraft complete with cockpit crew is a wet lease. A lease of an aircraft only, is a dry lease.

Foreword

This eminently readable book will appeal to all those with a real interest in aviation. The author, Brian Mercer, has spent a lifetime flying both military and civil aircraft, and in the following pages he recounts his experiences in a style that transports the reader into the exciting and exhilarating environment of the air; appealing to young and old alike and reflecting the author's passion for flying and his innate sense of humour.

The book is essentially divided into two parts: the first focuses on Mercer's 18 years with the Royal Air Force, whilst the second covers his 30 years as an airline pilot. I knew him well during the first period when we served together three times, notably with the RAF's famous Hunter formation aerobatic teams of Nos 111 and 92 Squadrons (the Black Arrows and the Blue Diamonds). Brian was an outstanding fighter pilot and squadron commander, leading by example and with a flair that earned both respect and admiration. It is not surprising, therefore, that he sees the highlight of his aviation career as his time in command of No 92 Squadron.

The author gives a vivid and accurate account of life in the RAF in the early post World War 2 period. He describes how it took some time for the rather gung-ho, live-for-today wartime fighter pilot culture, which was partially to blame for the RAF's relatively high accident rate of the 1950s, to evolve into one that was more measured and responsible, and, in my view, more effective. A further reason for the RAF's poor flight safety record at that time was the lack of experience on jet aircraft of many of the more senior pilots and flying instructors; some indeed finding it difficult to transition from high-performance piston-engined fighters such as the Spitfire and Tempest to the jet-engined Meteor and Vampire.

Mercer explains why formation aerobatics is an inherently risky flying activity requiring skill, aptitude and a highly professional approach by pilots involved. They must have self-belief and total trust in their fellow team members; they take pride in their corporate achievements, and they enjoy the accolades and camaraderie. In essence, their "esprit de corps" is strong and tangible. The author successfully conveys all of this and, through a liberal smattering of amusing anecdotes, that life in such a tight-knit unit is above all fun.

The author's view that the RAF rather lost its edge after WW2 by lagging behind the Americans in swept-wing fighter development – the RAF's Hunter entered service some 4 years later than the American F-86 Sabre – is fair. He is also right to be highly critical of the UK Defence Minister's assumption in 1957 (the kernel of Duncan Sandys' Defence White Paper of that year) that manned fighter aircraft would soon give way to guided missiles. As a result, the Mach 2 Hunter replacement (the Hawker P1121) and other advanced aircraft programmes (the P1154 and TSR2) were cancelled. This macro policy change proved to be a disaster – manned fighters and fighter bombers are still indispensable today, viz the two recent Gulf Wars - and set the RAF back many years; indeed, some would argue that it has not yet fully recovered.

The reader can almost sense the agonizing that Brian Mercer must have gone through in making his decision to leave the RAF when a brilliant career still stretched before him. Like many other RAF officers at the time, and since, he clearly felt unable to come to terms with spending more time as a staff officer than in the cockpit and in command. He thus chose to swap a "mahogany bomber" (a staff desk) for an airline flight deck, which presented a different set of challenges but which, from a fighter pilot's point of view, could reasonably be described as driving a bus rather than a Formula One racing car! That the author was able to adjust very well is clear from his narrative, for he rose from junior First Officer to be Manager of Cathay Pacific's 747 fleet. While the adrenalin may have flowed less often, the money and lifestyle were good, and most important, the buzz of performing to the highest standards in the air was still there. As this excellent book relates so well, I suspect that for Brian Mercer it always will be so; he is one of aviation's "elite".

Air Chief Marshall Sir Patrick Hine GCB, GBE, FRAeS

Introduction

My life in aviation spanned the years from 1946 to 1996 and this book is about what happened to me and my friends during that period. We are the forgotten generation; just too young for World War Two and just too old for the Falklands. We were the Cold War warriors and whilst most never had to shoot guns in anger, some of us did have moments of drama in such places as Malaya, Suez, Aden, the Oman and of course the big one – Korea. Significantly, Korea is now referred to as the forgotten war.

The RAF's involvement in Korea was small, but useful lessons were learned by those who flew on attachment to the American squadrons and No 77(F) Squadron of the Royal Australian Air Force, because only they had experience of Jet v Jet combat. Nevertheless, the F86s shot down the Mig 15s at the rate of twelve to one and their task did not compare with that of Johnny in his Spitfire or Hank in his Thunderbolt up against Fritz and Heinz in their Messerschmitts and FW190s. The German pilots were very good indeed, as were the Italians, despite what we were told at the time. But history is full of examples of brave and gallant men fighting for rotten causes.

Our main task in the fifties and sixties was to confront the projected mass assault on the United Kingdom by large numbers of Soviet bombers, some of which would be carrying atomic bombs. To counter this nightmare we would have to scramble a mass of fighters as rapidly as possible irrespective of the weather conditions. Training for this scenario in our jet fighters, which had very limited endurance and carried no worthwhile navigation aids, led to some very interesting moments. We had plenty of accidents and I find it amazing that we did not have more.

I thought that the life on a fighter squadron was wonderful. The squadron was like our family, it meant everything to us. The mess parties could get a bit wild particularly in the fifties but it should be noted that all our Station Commanders, Wing Leaders, Squadron Commanders and most Flight Commanders, were veterans of World War Two, so the wartime attitudes were still in vogue. The same attitude prevailed on the night fighter squadrons despite their "lone wolf" type of operation.

So for year after year we practised and trained; honing our skills at air combat and gunnery and took our turn at sitting in cold cockpits at the end of a runway, ready to scramble at the first sign of a mystery blip on the air defence radar. Scrambles were quite frequent but thankfully it was never the real thing.

For some time I was involved in international display flying as a leader or a member of a formation aerobatic team and that added considerable spice to life at the cost of extra stress. Display flying meant that we saw interesting places and now and again met exalted personages. I was glad that my parents were able to attend one of my investitures at Buckingham Palace to make up for the problems I gave them as a rather unhappy schoolboy. I was amazed by the Queen Mother when she gave me my first "gong". Despite the fact that I was about number three hundred in the queue, she knew exactly who I was and what I had done and she did not seem to have received any prior briefing.

There was a bit of fear now and then. When you are running out of fuel in bad weather and unsure of where the hell you are, those icy fingers start to dance up your spine. My periods of greatest tension used to occur just before a big air display. I remember at Furstenfeldbruck having to steady my right hand with my left to push the starter button. The funny thing was that as soon as the engine was running, all the tension vanished and I felt completely calm and in control.

Originally I intended to write only about the Air Force but then decided that Civil Aviation, particularly Cathay Pacific, deserved a chapter. Flying airliners is a job but flying fighters is more of a vocation and I hardly ever met anyone I did not like in the fighter world. Alas, I cannot say the same about the civil flying game where life is governed by the two S's: Seniority and Salary. But at least Cathay Pacific was more like the Air Force than any other airline I can think of.

I would like to thank my old friend and colleague Air Chief Marshall Sir Patrick (Paddy) Hine for writing the Foreword to this book. My thanks also to David Watkins for his help and encouragement and finally, to Sheila Moss for her typing and patience.

Brian P.W. Mercer
Araluen, Western Australia
2006

CHAPTER ONE

Early Years

I think it all started about 1935 when as a small child I was taken to an airshow by my father. It was probably in the Manchester area and very likely Alan Cobham's flying circus. I must have been five or six years old and remember little except for the noise, but one memory stayed with me. A small red biplane taxied very close to us and when the pilot climbed out of the cockpit, his leather jacket, white scarf and goggled helmet left a lasting impression.

I grew up during the depression of the 1930s in a small town in north-east Lancashire, Great Harwood. The town had been the abode of John Mercer, the inventor of mercerised cotton, a process which gave to cotton some of the qualities of silk. Consequently the town meeting place was the Mercer Hall and the central square contained a clock tower called the Mercer Clock. However, neither fame nor fortune had filtered down to my father's branch of the family from this distant relative.

My father was one of nine children. They were English Protestant stock with some Huguenot blood. They were also very poor. My paternal grandmother was a remarkable woman, for in addition to bringing up nine children, she was, by all accounts, a very accomplished cotton weaver.

Apparently she used to go to the mill at 6 a.m. and set up her looms; return home to give the children their breakfast, then return to the mill for a full day's work. I remember her as a large, kind woman with a very commanding presence and my father thought the world of her. He was the second youngest of the nine and the only one who went to university. My mother was an Irish Catholic from a town called Swinford in County Mayo. She came to England following the Great War, together with her sister, Cissie. They were both teachers. Mother was apparently something of a beauty in her younger years, with startling green eyes and jet black hair. Perhaps a distant ancestor had been a survivor of the Spanish Armada.

The mixed marriage meant that I was sent to a Catholic college and my sister, Aileen, to a girls' convent school. Mother was a staunch Catholic but father had a much more relaxed attitude towards religion and in general outlook was a true liberal. It seems that during the 'troubles' following the Great War, my Uncle Willie on my mother's side was a fringe member of the IRA whilst my Uncle Leonard, on my father's side, served for a while in Ireland as an auxiliary policeman, a 'Black and Tan'. Leonard had fought in Palestine as a trooper in the 11th Hussars and, unable to get a job after the war, had gone over to Ireland. Neither uncle seemed in the least bloodthirsty to me. Willie farmed in County Mayo and Leonard, after a variety of jobs, married a wealthy widow. Both of them lived to a ripe old age.

Father went to France in 1916 as a private in the Royal Engineers just in time for the Somme battles. He eventually became a staff sergeant and was the chief despatch rider at one of the army headquarters, I think General Plumer's

Second Army. Father was pretty lucky. He was never wounded but was gassed near Ypres and had to be invalided home for a while. He was talked out of joining the Royal Flying Corps by his mother, if she had not done so, the chances are that I would never have been born. He told me that he became so sick of the squalor of the ground war that the thought of a comfortable bed every night and escape from the never-ending bully beef and plum jam made the risk worthwhile. However, becoming a pilot in 1916/17 was only just short of committing suicide. Father had a lot of his old maps from the war and I have clear memories of his stories of that awful conflict. At the age of eight or nine, I knew about places like Ypres, Messines Ridge, the Menin Road and Passchendaele.

After the war my father obtained a BSc in Chemistry from Liverpool University and no doubt enjoyed a few years of batcherlorhood in the 'roaring twenties'. He had a rich friend, the scion of a cotton family, who owned an Hispano Suiza car. He told me that the two of them once averaged a speed of 60 mph from Blackpool to home, a distance of some 40 miles, and a remarkable feat in the early 1920s.

Our part of Lancashire was a pretty good place to grow up. We lived right on the edge of town just beyond the really affluent street, naturally called Park Lane. This was the area of the cotton barons and the successful businessmen and professionals. Between our home and my elementary school there were areas of terrible poverty during the years of the Depression and I remember one night watching a large gathering of unemployed men holding a meeting in the town square. We were in my Uncle Claud's flat over his insurance broker's office. There were speeches and banners, a lot of noise, but no violence, and when they dispersed the sound of the clogs which most of them wore made a deafening noise. Martin Cruz Smith, accurately described this sound as 'like a river of stones'.

Uncle Claud was nicknamed Bogie, I never knew why but suspect it was because he could never manage a par on any golf hole. Father was a keen golfer and I often went around with him and his Scottish friend, George Robson, a local doctor. From my bedroom window I had an uninterrupted view of Pendle Hill, made famous by the Lancashire witches of the seventeenth century. The western foothills of the Pennines are really very beautiful, and in my view compare very well with the Yorkshire Dales. I have happy memories of cycling all over the area with my friends and swimming in the River Ribble at Mitton and Sawley. This is the area of Whalley Abbey, Clitheroe Castle, Stonyhurst College, Ribchester (a Roman cavalry outpost) and the Forest of Bowland, which stretches north up to the Lake District. I also remember bonfire nights; that old terrorist Guy Fawkes bequeathed a lot of fun to the boys of my generation, like raiding other bonfires to pinch their wood and ambushing rivals with little red firecrackers called demons. Great fun, but I suppose that is all forbidden now.

Six days after bonfire night was Remembrance Day. I well recall the sombre looks, the cripples, the men with missing limbs and disfigured faces in the crowd gathered around the war memorial. We lived in an area of the 'pals' battalions'. In the small town of Accrington, not far away, there was street after street with no young men left after the First World War.

The park in my home town of about 8,000 souls has a war memorial containing hundreds of names, most of them from the Great War. Every Australian knows about Anzac Cove in Gallipoli, but how many British people know of Lancashire Landing just a few miles further south, where the Lancashire Fusiliers suffered 53 per cent casualties before they even reached the beach. The survivors still drove the Turks from the beach and established themselves ashore. British reticence has done a great disservice to the memory of our soldiers. A few years ago I had a discussion with an Australian about Gallipoli. He had no idea that any British soldiers had been there. I told him that the British lost 21,000 men, the French 10,000, the Australians 9,000, the New Zealanders 3,000 and the Indian Army 3,000. I didn't think he believed me. The British 29th Division, a first-rate division of regulars with Lancashire, Hampshire and Irish battalions was mathematically wiped out twice in the ill fated Gallipoli campaign.

On 3rd September 1939 the world changed. At the age of ten I listened to Neville Chamberlain's speech with my parents and could not understand why they looked so worried. In my ignorance and innocence I thought it was all terribly exciting and no thought that we could possibly lose the war entered my mind. To the children of my age it was all the Empire, 'Land of Hope and Glory', 'Rule Britannia' and that ludicrous song, 'We're going to Hang Out the Washing on the Siegfried Line'. I never heard my father sing that song. He and his generation knew just how hard it was to beat the Germans.

Our politicians had done it again. The army was small and badly equipped. The navy had no effective way to counter the inevitable U-boat offensive. Only in the air force was there a glimmer of hope, but even in the air we had a lot of catching up to do. But I was just a schoolboy trudging on foot and by bus to school every day. I did not really enjoy my schooldays. I was taught by Marist fathers some of whom did not spare the rod. They certainly did not generate any enthusiasm for learning. The only subject I really enjoyed was history which was taught by a Mr Earnshaw, our only lay teacher. The school's sporting facilities were poor; it was soccer or nothing. To my mind there was too much religion including an annual period of retreat; days of prayer and meditation – sheer torture for the average schoolboy. At the age of eleven I was told that to skip Mass on Sunday was a mortal sin and should I die before going to confession, then I would burn in hell forever. My mother actually believed this rubbish.

One day, amorous advances were made to me by a priest. He did not succeed, and he was not a member of the school faculty. I did not tell my parents; it would have devastated my mother. But my scepticism towards organized religion began to grow from that day. However, I am not anti-Catholic. The service padres I met later were mostly good men and the Catholic ones seemed more human and relaxed than their Protestant counterparts. In his autobiographical book on the Great War, *Goodbye To All That*, Robert Graves says that the only padres one saw where the bullets were flying, were the RCs.

School was accompanied by the blackout, sirens and air raids. We had great excitement one day. The siren sounded and off we jogged to the school air-raid shelter when right over our heads came a German bomber flying extremely low

– so low in fact that I could clearly see a helmeted German face in the nose, which seemed to be staring right at me. The next moment two Hurricanes came flashing over, and they shot him down in the Rossendale Valley just a few miles away. One night my mother stuck my sister and me under the heavy kitchen table when a stick of bombs went off fairly close. There was a factory that made Bristol aero engines not far away and if that was the target then they missed. This factory was surrounded by barrage balloons which were all destroyed in spectacular fashion one day by an electrical storm.

My father was teaching mathematics and science at a local grammar school during the war and also served as a special constable. Mother was doing some supply teaching and my sister was at her convent school. She did not enjoy it much but was more academically inclined that me and eventually obtained a degree from Leeds University.

I clearly remember standing on a hill one night with my father, listening to the sound of the German bomber engines and watching the glow of the fires from a raid on Liverpool. Cousin Donald was a fighter pilot, and flew Spitfires and other types over Europe and Burma. His brother Joe was in the Western Desert. He was an RAF radio apprentice and after a pretty exciting and uncomfortable war, ended up as a squadron leader signals officer. Cousin Arnie was in the USA learning to fly under the 'Hap' Arnold scheme. He ended up flying Mustangs and Spitfires but did not survive. Cousin Edna was a corporal in the WAAF at Biggin Hill and Uncle Arthur, who had been the radio officer on a White Star liner, was a radio instructor in the RAF. I could not wait to join them. Arnie was like the big brother I never had. He gave me my first ride on a motor cycle, his Scott Flying Squirrel, and also my first drive at the wheel of a car, on Southport Sands in his ancient Talbot. His father, my Uncle Fred, was rather cross about that because I was only ten at the time.

One day the Americans arrived, to the delight of the young women in our locality. The John Schlesinger film *Yanks* caught the atmosphere perfectly: trucks, jeeps and soldiers with a seemingly inexhaustible supply of chocolate bars and chewing gum. I arrived home one day with an American soldier I had met on the bus from school. He was a big, polite young chap from Michigan. I hope he survived Omaha Beach and Normandy.

At about this time I realized that if I wanted to get anywhere in my life then I had better get cracking with my school work. In my final year, instead of hovering round the bottom of the class, I moved up to about second. At the school prizegiving following matriculation, the headmaster wore a rather bemused expression as he presented me with a prize. Out of ten subjects, I had done very well in nine but had failed Latin. I could never see the relevance of this subject. I objected to being rapped over the back of my fingers with the edge of a ruler by the Latin teacher – a very painful experience that came my way often. Nevertheless, I can still say in Latin, 'These things having been done, the legions of Caesar crossed the river'! *Julius Caesar* was our Shakespeare piece for the final English literature examination, and to this day I can rattle off great chunks of the speeches of Caesar, Mark Anthony, Brutus and Cassius.

With the war over, to everyone's surprise I was accepted at the School of Architecture at Manchester University, four months before my seventeenth birthday. I thought the freedom of University life was marvellous after the stultifying atmosphere of school. I was actually allowed to talk to girls and drink beer in the students' union. Two friends of mine were Dutch and in their room was a large swastika flag which one of them had pinched from the roof of the Gestapo Headquarters in Rotterdam. Meanwhile I was learning all about the finer points of classical Greek architecture: Doric, Ionic and Corinthian columns, and pseudo-peripheral temples. At this stage one learned about form and design; the engineering bits were to come later. Before too long however, it became clear to me that I was not a very good draughtsman. I had recently joined the University Air Squadron (UAS), passed the medical and aptitude tests and was attending lectures on navigation, meteorology and aerodynamics in the evenings. Then one morning in January 1946, when I had just turned seventeen, I had my first flying lesson in a Tiger Moth at Barton Airfield. By the time we had climbed above the purple industrial haze into the clear blue sky, I was hooked. It was magic. Never mind that I was extremely cold (the rear cockpit of a Tiger Moth in the English winter is definitely not hot), this was what I wanted to do. I could not have known that I was going to spend the next forty-seven years doing little else.

I spent two weeks at an RAF Flying School near Wolverhampton in 1946. It was the annual summer camp of the UAS but I was not allowed to fly solo because of my age, which was a great disappointment. Shortly thereafter, following a rather disastrous attempt to design a public toilet for the town centre of Bolton, a project given to the students of my year, I went to see my professor and told him I wanted to join the RAF. Unsurprisingly, he thought that was a jolly good idea. There followed a frustrating delay, for the RAF did not want many new pilots at this stage. The Russians, however, were being increasingly difficult in Europe and Churchill had already made his famous 'Iron Curtain' speech in Fulton, Missouri. Eventually I was called for and had to go through the same medical and aptitude tests all over again. Finally I found myself pounding a drill square at Wilmslow as an aircraftsman second class, wondering when I would next see an aeroplane. Then someone remembered me and I was posted to the Aircrew Holding Centre at South Cerney, Gloucestershire.

It was an extraordinary period in the RAF which was still trying to reorganize itself following the post-war run-down. We were a diverse group at South Cerney. While most of us were little more than schoolboys, we also had an ex-Ghurka officer, an ex-Royal Navy deck officer and an ex-Seafire pilot who had been in the Pacific Fleet late in the war. There were two Australians and a Canadian who had worked their passage to England and an ex-warrant officer. In the group ahead of us there was even an ex-major from the Parachute Regiment. It did not matter who you were or what you had done or what rank you had held. All of us were lumped together as aircrew cadets living in barrack blocks and subject to the same discipline.

Eventually we were sent to a flying grading school at Shellingford, near Oxford, and for me this was a delightful interlude, flying Tiger Moths around the beautiful English countryside. Taffy Watkins-Jones, the ex-Seafire pilot, was excused this duty but Digger Ryde, who had got his wings with the Royal Australian Air Force (RAAF) at the end of the war, was not. My instructor was very impressed until I told him that I had done quite a few hours already with Manchester UAS. They let me fly solo and for the rest of the period at Shellingford my instructor seemed to concentrate on aerobatics and low flying which suited me fine.

After about three weeks we were back at South Cerney awaiting our fate, for depending on our performance at the flying grading school, we were to be trained as pilots, navigators or signallers. Our future was disclosed to us in a rather cold-blooded fashion. We were formed up on parade and in alphabetical order, were told our grading. There were some very disappointed faces on that parade. Young 'Rusty' Steele-Morgan was quite heartbroken to be told he was to be a navigator. We were to meet again. The RAF had reactivated the Rhodesian Air Training Group and we future pilots were to go to Southern Rhodesia and form No. 7 Course at Heany, just outside Bulawayo.

CHAPTER TWO

Initial Training

One winter's day, early in 1948, my companions and I boarded a Union Castle liner at Southampton and for the next three weeks lived the 'life of Riley' despite our miserable pay. We were in tourist class, but that seemed pretty luxurious after a military barrack block. There was an officer in charge of us but he was in first class, and as we all behaved ourselves, we hardly ever saw him. My Canadian pal, George Baldwin from North Bay Ontario, did not enjoy it much. He suffered dreadfully from seasickness despite the fact that he was one of the toughest young men I had ever met. He came back to life for a few hours when we called in at Madeira, a most delightful and picturesque island, but as soon as we set sail again, he resumed his quiet, pale-faced demeanour. (Poor George was to die four years later in the flaming wreckage of a Meteor.) The rest of us thoroughly enjoyed ourselves with deck games, fancy dress parties, dances, all the usual shipboard pastimes. Also on board was a group of young men going out to join the British South African Police, as the Rhodesian police force was known in those days, and a group of young nurses who were going to work in the hospitals of Salisbury and Bulawayo.

Other pals of mine in the group were Frank Wilson from Bolton, a classical music enthusiast and a champion beer drinker, Bob Cook and Bob Jacobs (who all eventually became BOAC captains); Vin Morgan, ex-Royal Marines, Neil Crighton-Smith, ex-Ghurkas, David Smith from the Royal Navy and Eric Gage, an ex-warrant officer. Eric was a lovely, even-tempered man. He must have been about twenty-eight and seemed very old to most of us. There was also Ralph Hancock from London. Years later I heard that he had been badly hurt in the crash of a Wellington trainer at advanced flying school.

Finally we arrived at Cape Town, tanned and fit, if several pounds heavier. The vista of Table Mountain before us was even more impressive than its photographs. The life of luxury was now behind us and we climbed aboard a train for the long journey up to Bulawayo. Many of our shipboard companions were on the same train. The journey lasted about three days and there were frequent stops to pick up fuel and water. At the night-refuelling stops there was usually a bonfire, surrounded by a group of Africans singing. This was the first time I heard the unique African harmony and I found it to be quite moving. We passed through Beaufort West, Kimberley, Mafeking and finally crossed over the Limpopo River into Rhodesia. After de-training at Bulawayo station we were transported to Heany by bus and shown into our barrack huts, which were very basic indeed and housed about twenty cadets. On that first evening in Rhodesia I became conscious of the particular smell of the African high country. Heany was about 4,500 ft above sea level. That African aroma was a faint and subtle mixture of woodsmoke and dust, and the memory stays with me today. For the next six months it was the same stuff again: navigation, meteorology, aero engines, aerodynamics, machine-guns, shooting rifles and pistols on the range – and drill, lots and lots of drill. We also had to play soldiers sometimes and march reasonable distances equipped with Lee Enfield rifles, tin hats and entrenching tools. We would dig a trench, jump into it, then jump out, fill in the trench and march home again. Meanwhile above us was the continuous drone of the Gypsy Major engines of the Tiger Moths and the snarling rasp of the Pratt and Whitney engines of the Harvards. The Harvards were referred to as the 'aloominum persoot ships' by the cadets.

We were all longing to get back into the air. The initial training went on for about six months and it felt like years. However, we had a good swimming pool and some tennis courts and I was fitter than at any other time in my life. The food was basic – plentiful but not good. We had a cadets' mess where we could buy beer and tastier, if less healthy, snacks. Some of the instructors would visit our little mess occasionally and entertain us with Second World War songs around the piano. I particularly remember Johnny Smith-Carrington and Phil Clay being good at this.

Finally the initial training phase was over and we were given two weeks' leave. Neil Crighton-Smith and I went to stay with a Rhodesian farmer and his wife on their tobacco farm near Salisbury. A lot of the farmers took in cadets, and their hospitality was much appreciated. One night Neil and I helped some farmers and their workers to put out a forest fire, so we were able to do something in return for the hospitality. On another day I went shooting with a farmer called Eric

Martin and shot a buck, but I felt so unhappy watching this beautiful creature die that I vowed never to shoot an animal again.

At last, back at Heany, it was time to go flying in the dear old Tiger Moth. I was introduced to my instructor, Flight Lieutenant 'Timber' Wood. I was told that he had flown Lysanders into French fields at night during the war, flying in secret agents and arms for the French Resistance fighters – a fairly hazardous operation. He had an unusual medal ribbon which was probably the Croix De Guerre. He and I got on very well. For several weeks it was circuits and landings, cross-countries, aerobatics, basic instrument flying, low flying and, now and again, illegal dog fights against other cadets, and I have happy memories of this period. Sometimes at weekends we would go into Bulawayo, where the rendezvous was the bar of the Grand Hotel and we would sometimes meet our instructors. They of course could afford to eat there, but we could not. However, at the bus stop was the famous Fritz with his food wagon. I can hear his voice now – 'Vun chicken roll und vun egg roll, Ja!' He was an institution. Poor Neil Crighton-Smith had fallen by the wayside on his Tiger Moth flying. He just could not land the thing properly. Fifty or 5 ft above the ground seemed the same to him. He was given extra time but it was no good and the poor chap was packed off home.

I came across him in Malaya some years later in an incredible coincidence. One night in 1956, I was telephoned to go immediately to the Tengah operations Room. Some communist terrorists were attacking a police post in north-east Johore and I had to lead a strike with four Venom fighter bombers to blast the area with rockets and cannon fire at dawn. Off we went at first light and did the job. That night I was at the cinema in Singapore and who should I run into but Neil Crighton-Smith, who was now not only an officer in the Malayan Police, but also the commander of the police post that had been under attack.

At the end of the Tiger Moth elementary flying stage, I went down to Johannesburg to stay with David Smith and his family. He had managed to get a transfer to the South African Air Force. He was a South African and being an ex-naval officer, had found the spartan living conditions at Heany a bit rough after a naval ward room. Jan Smuts and his Unionist Party had only just been voted out by Malan's Nationalists and South Africa was entering its unhappy time. However I had a very pleasant two weeks there and met some very nice people, one of whom lent me his BMW motorcycle.

Back at Heany it was time to fly the Harvard, A much more 'grown-up' machine, with its 550 horse-power engine, constant-speed propeller, flaps, retractable undercarriage and a cockpit full of instruments and switches. The ubiquitous Harvard was a very successful training machine. It was a delight to fly, but had a couple of vices that were enough to keep one on one's toes. It would swing into a 'ground loop' on landing if you were not careful and would flick into a stall if the airspeed got too slow during a turn. Anyone who could fly a Harvard should have no problem flying a Spitfire or a Mustang. The Australians built a version, which they called the Wirraway, and even made a stop-gap fighter out of it. One shudders to think of the poor devils who had to fight the Japanese Zeros in a Wirraway. The RAAF had a song full of black humour about this situation. The only part I remember describes the required action should you get a Zero on your tail: 'Do not hesitate, shove the throttle through the gate and blind the bastard with oil.'

My new instructor was Flight Lieutenant Jimmy Whitwick. He looked like a bank manager and was very precise and conscientious. There would be no low flying and chasing ostriches across the African plain with Jimmy. He was a very good instructor and taught me well. During my first solo in the Harvard I remember feeling that at last I was becoming a proper pilot. I was of course, quite mistaken about that.

At this stage of our training we were upgraded from the barrack huts to smaller buildings with just two cadets to a room, so life became a little more comfortable. I had also been introduced to a wealthy family who owned some large department stores in Rhodesia. One particular free weekend I was due to be picked up at the camp gate and taken out to the family farm for a couple of nights. For the first and only time, however, I was put on a charge for being thirty seconds late for a lecture. That seemed to be the end of the weekend, but I hatched a plot with my friend Ralph Hancock. For the princely sum of 10 shillings, he agreed to attend the compulsory defaulters' parade at the guardroom for the orderly officers' roll call. When the name 'Mercer' was called out, he was to shout 'Sir' in the approved military fashion. Unfortunately the orderly officer decided to inspect the defaulters' parade and Ralph earned me two extra days' 'jankers' for having dirty buttons. It was worth it but I was a bit cross about the 10 shillings.

A few of the ex-ground crew chaps had bought an old car which they rebuilt. It was an American Graham from 1934 or

1935 and four of us drove up to the Victoria Falls for a long weekend. We shared the driving because it was quite hard work driving on the dirt roads, which had two tarmac strips on which you kept your wheels. I found the Victoria Falls simply awesome. We were paddled across the Zambesi by a couple of locals and the angle of drift in the current was rather disturbing as the roar of the falls was very loud from just a little way downstream. The thought that the boatmen could lose their paddles was quickly banished from my mind. I remember standing within a few feet of a part of the falls called the Devil's Cataract. To have this vast quantity of water rushing down 400 ft very close to one's face was quite disturbing and the noise was deafening. We enjoyed two days of luxury at the Victoria Falls Hotel, then filled the car's fuel tank and set off for home, flat broke. Of course we ran out of petrol a few miles short of Bulawayo but were rescued by a Rhodesian farmer who kindly topped us up from a jerry can he had in his truck. The Rhodesians were all like that in those days and I never noticed the slightest hint of racial tension. I feel angry and sad about the situation today in what is now Zimbabwe.

We were coming to the end of the academic part of the flying training before moving to the final stage, which would involve night flying, formation flying, aerial gunnery, dive bombing and low-level bombing. There was one exercise which I remember as very sick-making. It was the closest I ever came to being airsick. Squadron Leader Joe Bodien, DSO, was in the front cockpit and I was in the rear under a hood and could not see out. The exercise was recovery from spins and unusual attitudes on instruments. After about half an hour of this, Squadron Leader Bodien flew back towards Heany, doing a series of barrel rolls. Eventually I had to call him over the intercom. 'Sir, one more barrel roll and I'm afraid I shall be sick all over the cockpit.' To my relief, straight and level flight was resumed.

For the advanced stage of training my instructors were Flying Officer Bell and Flying Officer Phil Clay, DFC. An ex-Spitfire pilot, Clay maintained the fighter pilot attitude and should one of my manoeuvres displease him, he would unfasten the control column from the rear cockpit and poke me in the back of the head with it. I enjoyed the dive bombing and low-level bombing which we did at the range at Mielbo up the railway line towards Gwelo, where there was an RAF navigators' school. Between Mielbo and Gwelo was a small place called Myasa. One cadet somehow got lost one day on a bombing exercise and flew too far up the railway line. This led to his dreadful pun. 'I obviously don't know Myasa from Mielbo.' Night flying was fun, although it was very dark on moonless nights over the African bush. Sometimes junior cadets hung about the holding point and cadged a night ride around the circuit in the back seat of a Harvard. I think there would have been a big fuss if the instructors had ever found out.

Finally it was all over. The last handling test, instrument flying test and navigation test were completed and those of us who had made it received our wings from Sir Godfrey Huggins, the Prime Minister of Southern Rhodesia. We were all very pleased with ourselves. My final flight at Heany was with Wing Commander Rump, the Chief Flying Instructor, on 15 September 1949, when he led a massed formation of

Harvards over Bulawayo for the Battle of Britain anniversary. Then it was away down the railway line again for a glorious week off in Cape Town before boarding the *Edinburgh Castle* for another fun-filled ocean cruise back to Southampton. Home again after a year and a half, fit, bronzed and happy to be home – even in rationed, socialist Britain.

CHAPTER THREE

Advanced Training

Following leave and a nasty bout of flu, I found myself back at South Cerney for a short bad-weather flying course on Harvards again. It was now December 1949. I was what was then called a P4 and on my sleeve wore a laurel device with one star in it. The Air Ministry had made a couple of strange decisions in that period. One was to get rid of the NCO's aircrew ranks of sergeant, flight sergeant and warrant officer. Instead they were P4, P3, P2, P1 or master aircrew. The more senior they were, the more stars they had in the laurel leaf. It was very unpopular and ground crew NCOs never knew who outranked whom in the sergeants' mess. Luckily this daft system did not last long and we reverted to the old ranks. The Air Ministry also changed the officers' uniform. The patch pockets disappeared and the tunic became plain-fronted, like a guardsman's parade dress. The classic RAF wings were replaced by a smaller version in gold thread. The whole ensemble looked wrong and was universally detested. This unpopular change was also reversed after a while.

At South Cerney I spent most of December in the back cockpit of a Harvard doing instrument flying and beam approaches at an airfield called Blakehill Farm. Just before Christmas I was given my White Card Instrument Rating and was allowed to take a Harvard up solo on my last flight and 'blow away the cobwebs' with a good session of aerobatics. Following a short break, I rejoined Vin Morgan at the Officers' Training School (OTS) at Spitalgate near Grantham. Out of twenty-eight of us who got our wings on the No. 7 Course at Heany, Vin and I were the only two who went to OTS, although several of the others were commissioned later.

Things were hotting up in Europe and elsewhere. The Berlin Airlift had already happened and before long the North Koreans were to attack the South and things became serious. Meanwhile for me it was lectures and more lectures, examinations and drill, drill, drill. How we all hated being screamed at by drill instructors! Finally it was over and I held the Kings Commission and was, officially at least, a gentleman.

At the end of April 1950, I found myself, together with Vin Morgan, at the Mosquito advanced flying school (AFS) at Brize Norton. I was about to enter a period of personal underconfidence, the only one I recall in my flying career. I have never understood why the RAF insisted that we had to switch off our engines and feather the propellers, or flame-out an engine, on a twin jet, in order to practise approaches and landings on one engine in a two-engined aircraft. Why not simply throttle back one engine? We killed far more expensively trained young men by this rule than were ever killed by the real event. In my view, it was a stupid rule for new pilots under training. Vin Morgan and I had been at Brize Norton for only a matter of minutes and were in conversation with a fellow No. 7 Course pilot who told us that Ron Lawson, a colleague from Rhodesia, had just been killed doing single-engined flying. He had got a bit too low and slow in his Mosquito with one propeller feathered and that was the end of him. The accident rate at Driffield, the Meteor AFS, was too high. Later there was an amazing accident at Middleton St George, another Meteor AFS. A young student pilot tried to overshoot on one engine with too low an airspeed and smashed through a car park, destroying his own car and demolishing his own room in the officers' mess. This building is now part of Teesside airport and locals say his ghost still haunts the corridors.

One morning I found myself walking towards a Mosquito with my instructor, Flight Lieutenant Charlie Watkinson. He was a kind soul and could sense my apprehension. I had never been in a twin-engined aircraft. I had not flown at all for months and in front of me was a 3,000 horse-power machine which I was going to have to master. At first all went well. The Mosquito was a delight to fly; it was much, much faster than a Harvard and turned out not to be too complex after all. But Charlie left after only two flights and I found myself in far less sympathetic hands. Frankly I found the instructors at No. 204 AFS generally aloof and unsympathetic. The Commander seemed all right. He was Wing Commander Mike Hunt, a Beaufighter and Mosquito ace from the Burma campaign. Vin Morgan, I know, felt the same way I did. After only four hours on the aeroplane I was doing single-engine approaches and landings with one propeller feathered. After six hours I was flying solo. After eight hours they gave me a navigator, Hamish Dewhurst from Manchester. I think Hamish was part-camel – he could drink vast quantities of beer and never seemed to need to go to the toilet.

'I was on Mossies during the War you know,' he said, adding, 'I was up at Charter Hall. We used to call it Slaughter Hall.'

Thanks Hamish I thought, that's made me feel a lot better!

On 4 May 1950, Hamish joined me in Mosquito Mark 6, No. 669. We were up for a session of practice circuits and landings. On about the fourth landing this aircraft really swung on me, the first and last time this ever happened. Following a normal 'tail-down wheeler' landing, the tail wheel touched down and the aircraft tried its usual trick of trying to go gently sideways. I corrected with rudder and the aircraft swung violently to the right – to this day I do not know why. Had I accidentally applied some right brake? Had the right tyre burst? I have absolutely no idea. We slid along the runway for a while with the left undercarriage collapsed and the left wing and propeller wrecked. The tower told us to get out as there was some fire. Hamish was quicker than me and accidentally kicked me in the head escaping through the top hatch whilst I turned off the magneto switches and fuel cocks. The Mosquito was a write-off but they were quite nice about it and got me into another one as soon as they could.

There was no more drama after that. The course proceeded normally: navigation exercises, lots of circuit practice and instrument flying, and plenty of single-engine approaches and landings. The Mosquito was a delightful machine, with wheels and flaps tucked away either on one or two engines. But in the circuit on one engine, it was a different story. As soon as you selected wheels down on the downwind leg, that big undercarriage slowly ground its way down because there was only one hydraulic pump working with one engine shut down.

The wheels were like two big dive brakes and you slowly lost height with them extended. The flaps were also slow to extend or retract with only one hydraulic pump in action. The recommended minimum height for executing a missed approach on one engine was 800 ft. With full power on one engine and a dead engine on the other side, the minimum control speed on a Mosquito was about 140 knots, the same as the Meteor jet fighter. Below this speed the rudder authority was insufficient to maintain control. In the RAF this was known as the 'critical speed'. (In civil aviation it is called Vm CA.) Steep climbs immediately after take-off were not recommended in a Mosquito because should you lose an engine before achieving 140 knots, then quite simply you were going to crash. It was a good idea to keep the initial climb very shallow until 160 knots, which was designated the 'safety speed'. The critical period was only a few seconds, but they were important seconds.

My ex-Rhodesia colleague Jimmy Dolittle lost an engine on a Mosquito night fighter just after take-off one night from Church Fenton and managed to survive by reducing the power on the live engine a little. He went for miles down the Vale of York just above the roof tops as his airspeed slowly built up. There was no rudder-boost system on the Mosquito or the Meteor and the effort required to hold in full rudder was enormous; after a while your knee would begin to tremble uncontrollably. All multi-engined civil airliners have a rudder-boost system and should it be found to be faulty during the pre take-off checks, then you cannot go until it is fixed. It is a mandatory item.

Towards the end of the Mosquito course, No. 204 AFS moved to Swinderby in Lincolnshire and we finished off our night flying using a satellite field at Wigsley. Wing Commander Mike Hunt did my final handling test and passed me, although I cannot believe he was very impressed by my flying. My next stop was the night fighter operational training unit (OTU) at Leeming in North Yorkshire.

One of the first things that happened at No. 228 OTU, was the crewing up of the pilots and navigator/radar operators (nav/rads). My nav/rad picked me, I suspect, because he thought I was the most socially acceptable of the available pilots. He was Flight Lieutenant Basil d'longh a former Second World War Liberator navigator. I invited him to come with me to Cousin Donald's wedding in Lancashire; all my female relatives thought he was gorgeous and declared he looked just like the Duke of Edinburgh. We got on well and for the next three months we were busy doing lots of practice interceptions using the Mark 10 Airborne Interception Radar, mostly at night, over the North Sea. We also did a lot of air-to-air firing against towed sleeve targets and I was glad to discover that I was good at that, because I was still not a confident Mosquito pilot.

Two rather dramatic events occurred at Leeming during this period. A young pilot who was, I understand, a former Sword of Honour winner at Cranwell, got a bit low on the approach and hit a bread van on the Great North Road. Apparently there were loaves scattered all over the place. However, it was not a bit funny because the poor pilot lost a leg. A flight lieutenant navigator who had been crewed with a young sergeant pilot approached the powers-that-be and said he refused to fly with him any more because he did not think he was safe. There was a big fuss and a court martial was threatened. I do not know what happened about that, but perhaps the navigator had a valid point, as I will explain later in the book.

At last the long, long training was over, after the best part of three years. Basil and I were posted to No. 29 Night Fighter Squadron based at West Malling in Kent.

CHAPTER FOUR

Night Fighters

Our first impression of West Malling was not good. We were interviewed by the Station Commander, who spent a few minutes threatening us with dire consequences if we did not behave perfectly in all respects. It was a most unfriendly welcome. The greeting from the squadron was much better, although I felt a bit of a prune when I walked into the crew room wearing the minuscule stripe of a pilot officer and saw before me a mass of medal ribbons. However, there was young Sergeant Navigator 'Rusty' Steele-Morgan, whom I had last seen on the parade at South Cerney when the grading school results were announced. The commanding officer (CO) was Squadron Leader Mike Shaw, DSO, an ex-Coastal Command ace and a very nice man. The two flight commanders were Ian Meiklejohn and Hugh Tudor, two strong-minded men who cordially detested each other, as I was to learn later. However, I liked them both. Flight Lieutenants Pete Needham and Bob Gellard were a great pair, with a wonderful sense of humour. Then there was Captain 'Terrible Tom' Trammel and his nav/rad, Top Sergeant Motil, both on exchange from the US Marine Corps. I immediately felt at home.

There was only time for a check flight with the CO and a sector recce with Rusty when on 2 October 1950, the whole squadron flew down to Tangmere for two weeks for the big air defence exercise of that year, Exercise Emperor. What can one say about Tangmere? The best and the happiest station in the whole of the RAF. The Station Commander was Tom Pricket, the Wing Commander Flying was Barney Beresford and the other squadron was No. 1 Fighter Squadron with brand new Meteor 8s.

We also learned that within a month we were to return to Tangmere on a permanent basis. Joy was unconfined, as they say. What was more, suddenly I found I could fly the Mosquito properly. There was no more apprehension, no more poor landings and the take-offs were all arrow straight. It had taken me just over 100 hours on type to master it. With hindsight I think that the jump from the Harvard to the Mosquito was just a bit too far, particularly as I was out of current flying practice. A few hours first in something like an Airspeed Oxford would have been a good thing.

Exercise Emperor was like the Second World War without live ammunition. For example, on 14 October, we were sitting in a dispersal hut around midnight when the order came to scramble. Off with the red goggles, jog to the aircraft, grab the bottom of the radiator in the wing leading edge and swing the legs through the small side door. Scramble into the seat and fasten the preadjusted parachute and seat harness. On with the magneto switches and pitot heater. Oxygen on, radio and helmet on. No priming required, the ground crew had prewarmed the Merlins. Thumbs up from the ground crew. Press the starter and booster coil buttons. The fuel cocks are

already on. Whine, cough, roar. No. 1 engine is running. Side
door is shut. Navigator warming up the AI radar and Gee box.
Another roar as No. 2 engine is started. Trims are preset.
Uncage the directional gyro. Off down the taxiway to the
runway threshold. Magnetos and pitch controls have been
checked earlier. Take-off clearance is given. Elapsed time
from scramble call, about four minutes. Rolling-start take-off,
120 knots, we are in the air. Hold her down a bit to achieve
safety speed. 'Gear up' to navigator. Acknowledged by him as
he raises the gear lever.

'Hello Shortfrock, Moonlight 16 Airborne.'

'Roger Moonlight 16, Vector Two Five Zero Make Angels
Twenty.'

'Roger Shortfrock, Vector 250 Angels Twenty.'

There was a loud squealing noise in my headset. Then from
me on the intercom.

'Christ Basil, I can only just hear him. They're jamming the
VHF'

We climbed up over the Channel following the distorted
instruction from the (GCI) radar station at Sopley and were
told to turn north. We reached 20,000 ft and Basil pointed to
the B scope on his radar. It was a mass of snow. The bombers
were throwing out window, (aluminium strips to jam the night
fighter's radar). Suddenly, 'Target, twelve o'clock, five miles.
Then 'Target moving right, now one o'clock, three miles
seven degrees up.' So it went on as we got closer and closer.
The instrument lighting was on minimum illumination and I
had the gunsight graticule so dim it was only just visible.
Suddenly I saw four pinpoints of light from a bomber's
exhausts; probably a Lancaster closed in to about 200 yards

and theoretically gave him a four second burst from the four Hispano cannons at no deflection. Basil then flicked our navigation lights on and off a few times. The startled rear gunner flashed his torch at us to signal that he was firing. 'Too late mate, you've had it,' I thought to myself. We repeated this twice more. By the third 'kill' we were just west of London.

While the innocent Londoners were sleeping below, a big bomber stream was flying over. No aircraft had any lights on. Into this bomber stream at least six Mosquito squadrons were vectored by the radar stations. The fighters were not showing any lights either – and it was peace time!

The tail gunners never saw us in time. Later I became rather cruel and used to turn on my landing lights after 'firing'. That must have made them jump. The German night-fighter aces Lent, Schnaufer and the Prince zu Sayn-Wittgenstein are reputed to have shot down about 300 night bombers between them and I believe it. We went back home to Tangmere, joined the circuit on the downwind leg and touched down gently after a curved approach. Red-eyed from staring through the windscreen, I entered the dispersal hut with Basil and swapped 'war stories' with some of the other crews. I would have loved a beer, but it was 3 a.m. Later the word filtered through that a Belgian air force night fighter had collided with a bomber in the Thames Estuary area. There are not expected to be any survivors. I sometimes get cross when I hear people sneeringly refer to the boring fifties. They were certainly not boring for me.

At the end of Exercise Emperor we returned to West Malling but within a month we were back at Tangmere permanently. My enthusiasm was temporarily dampened when I was 'volunteered' to check the officers' mess inventory – a rather daunting task made much easier for me by the assistance of dear old Billy Barrel, the Mess Manager and the sterling duo of Mr Gooch and Mr Gurney, two old batmen who had been at Tangmere for years. I was for some time trapped in a world of 'pots, chamber, chairs ladderback, blankets, grey wool' etc. During the course of this marathon I discovered a marvellous RAF form. It was Form 21, known as a Conversion Voucher. Should you be short of one 'pot, chamber' but had a surplus 'blanket, grey wool', you could swap one for the other. A lot of that went on during the course of my inventory check. It seemed to me that if one lost a Mosquito it would be possible to swap it for 'one chair ladderback' if they happened to be on the same inventory, and everyone would be happy. But, perhaps that was being a bit naïve.

This was a happy time. On some mornings, walking from the mess after breakfast, I would reflect on how lucky I was to be doing what I loved in a terrific place with so many nice people around me. The pay was not good (it never was before Margaret Thatcher) and a good third went on my mess bill, but nevertheless, life was great.

In addition to lots of practice interception exercises we also carried out plenty of air-to- air and air-to-ground gunnery. The cannons were under the cockpit floor in the Mosquito, and when they were fired the cockpit filled with cordite fumes. One day I went air firing; my No. 2 was the sergeant pilot who had been the subject of the controversy at Leeming some months earlier. We were shooting at a sleeve target towed by a Martinet aircraft at about 2,000 ft over the Channel, and the two of us were making alternate attacks. Suddenly the Sergeant was no longer to be seen. He had simply flown into the sea just a few miles south of Bognor Pier. I did not witness the crash, so had no idea how or why it had occurred, but that was the end of him and of the young navigator in his cockpit.

One day we had a very interesting squadron visit to the Saunders Roe factory on the Isle of Wight, where we were able to inspect the almost complete Princess flying boat. This huge machine looked magnificent: there was a staircase between decks and the flight deck was so big it looked like a ship's bridge. Unfortunately flying boat operations no longer made economic sense and after an impressive debut at the Farnborough air show the project was cancelled. The romantic era of long-range flying boat journeys was over.

By 1951 our Mosquito 36s were getting a bit long in the tooth and we exchanged them for some Mk 30s. There seemed to be no difference as far as I was concerned. This Second World War machine was still effective against piston-engined bombers but jet bombers would be coming into service soon and against them the Mosquito did not have a hope. However, I recall that one night we were able to catch an American B-50 Superfort at 33,000 ft. This was not too comfortable in an unpressurized cockpit and my abiding memory is of the extreme cold; I had to scrape ice off the inside of the windscreen. Basil needed to pee on this flight. We had a tube device for this purpose, but it was frozen up, so I collected most of it in my right flying boot. Basil was quite mortified.

In 1951 Tangmere was visited by the West German defence minister, which seemed quite strange only six years after the war. We did a formation display with about twelve Mosquitos and on the second fly past we all had our port engines stopped, with the propellers feathered. The formation leader then called, 'Unfeather port go.' Something made me glance to the right and I saw my navigator's index finger poised over the starboard feathering button! I lashed out with my right hand and just in time knocked his hand away. We came very close to having an engineless Mosquito at only 400 ft above the ground.

One day someone decided we were to try some head-on attacks against a formation of B-29s. This was a most sobering experience and it was not repeated. I think the bomber crews got more frightened than we did. There were a couple of other jolly exercises given to us in 1951. On one of them we were to intercept a Coastal Command Lancaster flying very low over the Channel; I think he was at about 250 ft and it was a very dark night. We had a radio altimeter and I set the red warning light at 100 ft. The Lancaster was simulating a mine-laying aircraft. When the red light flashed ON my pulse rate leaped as I heaved back on the control column. However, we did manage the interception. I believe one of the Coltishall squadrons lost a crew on one of these capers.

Another jolly idea some one came up with was to use fighters to attack small surface craft at night. Surely the German E-boats were not coming back! A motor torpedo boat (MTB) would control a small vessel which was the target. Coastal Command would find the target boat with their ASV radar and drop flares, and then the Mosquitos would attack it with their cannons. I never did one of these, but Basil and I went out on the MTB one night. The high-speed run out from Portsmouth Harbour was great but the return voyage was not. Of course the radio control broke down and we had to tow the target boat back at about 4 knots through the channel chop, which was very sick-making. I had to go topside, as I would have been sick if I had stayed below.

My boss, Mike Shaw, called me into his office one morning and asked me if I was interested in a permanent commission (at that time I held an eight year short service commission), of course I said I was – perhaps someone had been impressed by my dexterity with the Form 21. After an interview with Group Captain Tom Prickett, I found myself before the Air Officer Commanding (AOC), Air Vice Marshal the Earl of Bandon, who had just taken over 11 Group. The interview must have been satisfactory because shortly thereafter I was awarded a permanent commission.

Mike Shaw left for another job and was replaced by, of all people, Squadron Leader Joe Bodien from Rhodesia days. He had been flying A-26s with the Americans in Korea where the Korean war was well under way by now. Hugh Tudor and Ian Meiklejohn had both left and I had a new flight commander, Major David Thomson of the US Marine Corps, who arrived with his nav/rad, Top Sergeant Larry Fortin. He had rows of medal ribbons from the war in the Pacific; he had flown Grumman Wildcats and Hellcats from the Guadalcanal campaign right through the other blood-soaked islands. We got on well. He had a little trouble landing the Mosquito for a while. We used to watch his kangaroo hops with some amusement and he would stalk into his office muttering about the 'goddamn airplane'. However, he soon got the hang of it.

After a few weeks he attempted to imbue us with that surprisingly formal American military protocol in the following manner: 'Right you guys. That's enough of this Dave shit. I'm a major and from now on you bums are gonna call me SIR!' We thought that speech was a scream.

Then came great news: we were to get jet night-fighters, the first squadron in the RAF to do so, perhaps even the first in the world. Down from Biggin Hill came Flight Lieutenant Fred Doherty with a Meteor 7, and in a remarkably short time he had checked us all out. I got two thirty-minute dual instruction flights, and that was my jet conversion. We were also given a Meteor 7 and a Meteor 4 to practise on for a while. Jet flying is 'old hat' now, but what a quantum leap in performance it was: the incredibly high indicated airspeeds, the amazing rate of climb, the smoothness and silence. Most surprising of all, compared to a Mosquito it was a piece of cake to fly. Landing speed was almost identical but the tricycle undercarriage made life so much easier.

The Mosquito remained our operational aeroplane for another four months but finally the Meteor NF 11s arrived in July 1951. They were built by Armstrong Whitworth and seemed well made and nicely finished. Now we could fly just as fast as No. 1 Squadron. From my logbook I see that we were operating both types for a while as the Meteor NF 11 complement slowly built up but it did not seem to cause any problems. No longer did Basil sit next to me on my right; he now sat behind in his own 'office' with his radar and navigation equipment.

My last couple of flights in a Mosquito were fairly memorable. On the air test all the cowling on the starboard engine came off. It flew fine but that naked Rolls Royce Merlin looked very funny. On the last flight, a delivery to the maintenance unit at Silloth in Cumberland, I had a total hydraulic failure and ended up doing a flapless landing with no tail wheel, which just scraped the paint on the back of the fuselage. Flight Lieutenant Jock Cassels, DFC, had joined the squadron. He had flown Mosquito bombers with the Light Night Striking Force during the war and that surely must have been one of the best jobs in the war. He had, however, belly landed a Mosquito on one engine into a Swedish field one night, so perhaps the job was not all that easy.

Mess life at Tangmere was terrific, we used to play silly games on dining-in nights. Many of them had an element of danger but the craziest was jousting. The swing doors in the long corridor were fixed open and at each end of the corridor was a fighter pilot with a bucket on his head, sitting on a bicycle with a mop positioned like a knight's lance. On the word 'Go' the two idiots would ride towards each other, the aim being to knock the opponent off his bike with the mop. No one was killed, but occasionally the medical officer would escort someone to sick quarters for running repairs.

Dave Thomson and his wife Patsy were very kind to me during this period. Both Dave and Larry Fortin, his navigator, owned huge American cars which they had shipped over, though how Larry survived driving in England I shall never know. Every time I was with him he headed straight for the wrong side of the road in his left-hand-drive Detroit monster. The meals that Patsy prepared at their rented home were tremendous, made, as they were, from the best supplies from an American PX. Food rationing was still in force in England, even five years after the end of the war.

An amusing incident occurred in the mess anteroom one day. It was just after lunch and the room was full of administrative officers quietly resting or reading their newspapers, when in came two young Thomson boys aged about seven and six, both dressed in full cowboy regalia. The two lads then opened fire with their cap pistols at the dozing officers. I would have loved to witness the scene. No doubt a letter was received by their father from the president of the mess committee concerning the incident.

About once a year all aircrew had to participate in an escape and evasion exercise. We were dropped off at night from the back of a covered truck in the middle of nowhere and expected to find our way to a rendezvous point, usually close to base and up to 50 miles from the drop-off point. Our enemies were the army and the local constabulary and if we were caught, it could prove most uncomfortable. I was caught just north of the South Downs on my first exercise and ended up in a cell, hungry, thirsty and wet through after fording a small river. I was interrogated several times and suffered petty inconveniences; blankets and pillows were taken away. The whole experience was so unpleasant that I was determined never to be caught again – and I never was. Some of the escapees showed considerable initiative. Cash was hidden in socks and pleasant nights were spent in country inns until finally a comfortable taxi took them to the rendezvous point. I heard of one pair who were apprehended driving along in a 'borrowed' steam traction engine.

We had a visit on one occasion from the Portuguese air force, flying Hawker Hurricanes of all things. They had been invited so that a film company could get some shots for that excruciatingly bad film about the Battle of Britain, *Angels One Five*. They were nice fellows but the whole mess smelled of their hair pomade for days. They were surprised to witness the behaviour of the British officers following the loyal toast after dinner on a guest night. Wing Commander Barney Beresford, the president of the dinner, stood up and called for a little more decorum; he was immediately struck on the head with a peeled banana. To give the Portuguese pilots their due, they joined in the fun and games themselves later on.

Various units were called to the colours as a result of the Korean War. The Florida Air National Guard squadron passed through with their A26 Invaders. Most of them seemed to be dentists, lawyers, etc and were none too pleased with their lot. A Vampire auxiliary squadron also joined us for a while from Llandow. 'Finest fighter squadron in Wales, boyo,' they said; they were of course, the only one.

Then we got the Meteor auxiliary squadron from Lancashire, led by Squadron Leader Jazz Storey, who used to wake his pilots up for breakfast by blowing on a hunting horn. They all owned water pistols and went about squirting everybody. It was irritating, but I have to admit that if one has a loaded water pistol, the temptation to use it is almost irresistible. On 111 Squadron in 1954, we also went through the same irritating phase.

The happy times continued at Tangmere, with parties in the mess bar with Dickie Dickinson, Mac McCaig and Ted Willis of No. 1 Squadron. Dickie managed to set his head on fire one night with lighter fuel but we put it out and no permanent damage was done. Ted Willis took off one day in a Meteor 8 that had not been refuelled. The engines, of course, stopped and Ted had to belly-land in a field; the 'brass' were pretty cross with him about that. Unfortunately he did the same about three years later, flying a Vampire out of Hong Kong with No. 28 Squadron. He tried to dead-stick back into Kai Tak but got it just a bit wrong and was killed when he collided with a hut on the airfield.

On 11 March 1952, I had my first trip to Germany. Joe Bodien led Sandy Mutch and myself to Gutersloh. We stayed for four days and did two night flights to give the 2nd Tactical Air Force radar controllers practice at controlling jet night fighters. The mess at Gutersloh was one of Göring's permanent *Luftwaffe* bases and was equipped with a couple of unusual features. In the washroom was a row of high basins and above each was a large padded button. The idea was to rest your forehead against this button to flush the basin whilst you were being sick. The other really odd thing was the joke room. An unsuspecting guest would be positioned in a certain place, then a secret button was pressed and a rather heavy beam fell on the guest's head.

The fellows at Gutersloh on the two Vampire squadrons were feeling annoyed. Gin had just gone from 2 pence to 3 pence a shot and whisky had gone up to 4 pence. We felt no sympathy for them whatsoever.

On 18 March 1952, five days after returning from Germany, Basil and I had a rather nasty experience. We were airborne at night intercepting some American B-50s out over the Western Channel. Major Thomson was also flying that night. The weather at Tangmere was not good and it started to become worse with a low cloud base and a misty drizzle. We were recalled to base, although we should really have been diverted to somewhere like Manston whilst still at high altitude. There was no real cause for worry; the GCA controller at Tangmere, Flight Lieutenant Victor Emmanuel Azarro, DFM and bar was first rate. Dave Thomson landed first and the visibility was so poor that a Landrover had to guide him back to dispersal. Part of the problem was that the windscreen demisting on the Meteors at that stage was virtually non-existent.

Then it was our turn and the GCA was not available. If my memory serves me correctly it had broken down. Basil navigated us in using Gee and the reflections of Chichester Cathedral and the Tangmere hangars on his airbourne interception (AI) Radar. The easterly runway was in use that night which did not have proper approach lighting, just some sodium lights on poles. I could not see the runway at all on the first approach and we had to overshoot. Our fuel situation was now critical. If we could not land from the next approach then we would have to climb up a little and bale out, and that could be hazardous because the Meteor night fighter had no ejection seats. I was flying solely on instruments throughout this – outside the cockpit was only blackness. Just to the left of the windscreen, there was a thick perspex panel called the direct vision (DV) panel measuring about 9 × 3 in. I opened this so that my left eye could peep out, but it did not help much and the noise was deafening. In we came again with wheels and flaps down. At about 300 ft I saw the glow from the sodium lights through the drizzle. Then at about 100 ft a few runway lights came into view. I slowly eased back the throttles and flared just a little. We were right on the runway centre line but just a few yards short and there was an almighty bang as the unchamphered edge of the runway ripped off the nosewheel and we slid down the runway on the nose and the main wheels, with our tail in the air. The aircraft was not badly damaged and flew again after a few weeks. The accident investigation fellows assessed the reason for the accident as 'pilot error under difficult circumstances', which I thought was pretty harsh. It is, after all, rather difficult to land an aircraft when you cannot see. The windscreen misting problem was solved later by the installation of a perforated 'piccolo' tube that ran around the side of the cockpit and under the windshield. Warm air bled from the engine circulated inside this tube and blew out of the holes. One day in a Meteor just after take-off, I pushed the lever which pressurized the cockpit; raw fuel squirted out of all the holes in the piccolo tube and I got drenched in kerosene. A ground engineer had installed a valve the wrong way around.

The pleasant life at Tangmere continued for another five months. Basil d'longh left for the US Air Force testing airfield at Eglin and after that most of my flying was with Flying Officer Mac McLean, Flight Lieutenant Bob Franks or Top Sergeant Fortin. On one night exercise with McLean in the back seat, we managed to intercept six Lincolns, one after the other. On another night whilst working with the (GCI) station at Sopley, I thought the voice of the fighter controller sounded very familiar; It was Cousin Donald, who was in the Auxiliary Air Force. He visited Tangmere a couple of days later and I was able to give him a ride in a Meteor NF 11. He found the performance very impressive after his last machine, a Spitfire Mark 8.

Joe Bodien left and was replaced by Squadron Leader Peter Horsley fresh from Buckingham Palace, where he had been a royal Equerry. His gentlemanly manner was in sharp contrast to the earthy style of Joe Bodien. One morning he came up to me and said, 'Well Brian, your tour is about over, what would you like to do next?' I told him I would like to get into single-seat day fighters and he said he would see what he could do.

It was now August 1952, a wonderful time to be on the Sussex coast but it was time to say farewell to the beach at West Wittering, the Unicorn in Chichester and the Old Ship at Bosham. No more Friday evening runs down to Brighton in the squadron car, a 1928 Rover. I had done my last low-level jaunt down the south coast beaches in the station Tiger Moth waving at pretty girls in bathing suits. Many years later, as a civilian, I visited Tangmere; it was almost deserted. There were no more aircraft of course and as I looked at the ivy-covered officers' mess and gazed up at the window of my old room, I was overcome by a tremendous feeling of nostalgia. How I wished I could start all over again.

CHAPTER FIVE

Day Fighters

Thanks to Peter Horsley, in August 1952 my wish for day fighters was granted and I found myself on No. 56 Squadron at Waterbeach, a few miles north of Cambridge. The Waterbeach wing, Nos. 56 and 63 Squadrons, was commanded by Wing Commander Paddy Barthrop and the station commander was Group Captain Arthur Donaldson. Our aircraft were Meteor 8s.

These were halcyon days for Fighter Command. We had wings of fighters all over the UK: Tangmere, Odiham, West Malling, Biggin Hill, North Weald, Duxford, Waterbeach, Wattisham, Church Fenton, Linton-on-Ouse, Horsham St Faith, Coltishall, Leuchars, etc. There were also about twenty Auxiliary Air Force squadrons, all flying Meteors or Vampires. There was a Canadian wing at North Luffenham and American squadrons at Bentwaters, Woodbridge, Shepherds Grove, Wethersfield and Manston. On the big annual air defence exercises, the sky over eastern England and the North Sea was full of aircraft and condensation trails. The build-up following the start of the Korean War had almost reached its peak. We also had many fighter squadrons in Germany and the Near and Middle East; we even had five in the Far East, in Malaya, Singapore and Hong Kong.

There was one problem, however. The arrival of the American F-86 Sabre had made every single one of our day fighters obsolete. The Americans had gone for swept wings and axial-flow engines. We had stayed too long with straight wings and centifrugal compressors. The death of Geoffrey de Havilland in the Swallow had frightened the establishment and, as I understand it, a very senior civil servant had decided that the sound barrier was impenetrable. The DH 108 Swallow was a tailless high-speed research aircraft designed to evaluate the handling characteristics of swept wing aircraft. Geoffrey de Havilland was killed on 27 September 1946 when the machine suffered a catastrophic structural failure at Mach 0.9. On 9 September 1948 the third prototype exceeded the speed of sound in a shallow dive and it was the first jet powered aircraft to do so. (The earlier American supersonic flights had been done in rocket powered machines.) All three of the Swallow prototypes crashed, killing their pilots. A very promising design, the Miles M52, had been cancelled in February 1946 by the Labour government in the interests of economy. It was decided to continue the investigation of supersonic flight by the use of models, but this was a failure and so the slight lead we had gained was then lost. We never recovered from these decisions and, since then, have always lagged behind the Americans in the development of fighter aircraft, with the exception of the brilliant Harrier. These fateful decisions were of course reversed, but we had lost too much ground. We fighter pilots were longing for the arrival of the Supermarine Swift and the Hawker Hunter, the development of which seemed to be taking for ever, although by today's standards it was actually quite quick. In the early fifties we really thought the Russians might very well roll through Western Europe. There were only two areas in which we could outdo the Americans. All our fighters were equipped with four 20 mm Hispano cannons which were superior in hitting power to the American 0.5 in Browning machine-guns. We were also braver when it came to bad-weather flying, to be frank, we were a bit too brave on occasions.

There were some real characters at Waterbeach. The mess was full of young, single officers, very different from today, when so many of the officers live out of mess and so many are married. There was Dennis Tann who could play the piano exactly like George Shearing, and one of the great characters, Flying Officer Alan Harvey – 'Ole Harve'. He was a very press-on pilot, a natural comic and a pretty good song-and-dance man. He bore a striking resemblance to the entertainer Roy Castle. He must have the record for the most extra orderly officer duties in the history of Fighter Command. In the mess corridor outside the bar was a glass case containing the uniform of the late Captain Albert Ball, VC. The holy of holies for 56 Squadron. One night the station commander came into the bar to see Harve decked out in Albert Ball's Royal Flying Corps uniform, doing one of his song-and-dance acts. Result: one week's orderly officer.

On 11 December 1952, Harve was my wing man when we got into a dog fight off the Suffolk coast with some American F-86s. The Americans became bored with their high-speed dives and zooms and decided to slow down a bit and mix it up, something they would never have been foolish enough to do in a real war situation. Thanks to our superior rate of turn and better acceleration, we got some good camera-gun shots.

Then Harve called out, 'Red Two, I'm running out of fuel.' He shut off one engine, pulled up his fuel balance cock to feed all the remaining fuel to the live engine and carried out a single engined landing at a disused wartime strip at Eye. The runway was covered in stones and small pot-holes but he landed without even scratching the paint. Sitting in the cockpit wondering what to do next, he was approached by a Suffolk local. According to Harve, the conversation went something like this.

Harve: 'Good morning, can you tell me where I am?'
Local: 'Arr, this be Oie.'
Harve: 'Yes, I know you are you, but where are we?'
Local: 'Arr, this be Oie airfield.'

Then the penny dropped.

Meanwhile, I had landed back at Waterbeach with at least four minutes' fuel left. I explained the situation, received a good ticking off from Paddy Barthrop and was ordered to proceed to Eye with a fuel bowser and a truck load of airmen. We spent a couple of hours cleaning up the runway, refuelling and inspecting the aircraft. I then flew the Meteor back to Waterbeach. Result for Harve: one week's orderly officer.

On another occasion Harve decided he would like to visit the Farnborough Air Show. He had no transport, so decided to borrow a car belonging to a pal, Dave Parry of No. 63 Squadron, who was away, assuming that Dave would not mind. The car was a typical vehicle for a fighter pilot of those days, an open Austin Seven from about 1935. Meanwhile, Dave returned and came to the not unreasonable conclusion that his car had been stolen and informed the police. Two constables in their Wolsley police car saw the car pass them and set off after it. Harve, who was blissfully unaware of any problem noticed the police car approaching from behind with bells ringing. It passed, waved him down and came to a halt. Harve then applied his brakes, which promptly failed, and he rammed the back of the police car. I believe there were conversations between the station commander and the Chief Constable. Dave Parry, of course, did not press charges. Result: two weeks' orderly officer.

No. 56 Squadron had three different COs during my time with them. I got on best with Scott Vos, a large South African; our paths would cross again some years later. He had been in the Western Desert in the early days of the Second World War and had flown against Italian Fiat CR42 biplanes in a Gloster Gladiator. My flight commander was Captain Jack Bodie, on exchange from the USAF. He was ex-West Point and a dedicated, conscientious officer. In spirit he remained very West Point: Impeccable uniform, erect posture and the cap always worn low and square like a guardsman on parade. He was very different from us but much respected for his integrity. He was also very religious and I later heard that he had become some sort of flying missionary in South America.

I was considered a bit unusual myself. To go from night fighters to day fighters was the reverse of the usual procedure but my extra experience in bad weather and instrument flying was to serve me well. We sometimes operated large groups of aircraft in very poor weather. No. 56 Squadron had lost a pilot just before I joined, when his canopy had come off while he was flying very fast at low level. Through some aerodynamic quirk it had taken his head off.

I remember one day lining up at the back of the whole wing for a wing scramble and snake climb exercise. The weather was atrocious, low cloud, base about 300 ft and with fairly heavy rain. As the pairs of Meteors rolled at three second intervals, visibility reduced to virtually nil in water spray. Shortly after I commenced my take-off roll with my number two in formation, I saw a bright orange glow ahead of me. One aircraft had slammed his ventral fuel tank back on the runway. He had hit someone's jet wash as he retracted his wheels. Out of the corner of my eye I saw him turning downwind, very low, with flames streaming from the ventral tank, but he got down all right. We finally broke into the clear at about 38,000 ft and joined up together. The rest of the flight was entirely taken up in recovering the wing as we descended in pairs for GCA approaches and formation landings two by two. The whole thing was ridiculous. No. 63 Squadron lost a pilot on one of these wing scrambles when he lost his leader in cloud shortly after take-off and crashed, presumably through disorientation.

Billy Drake, the Linton-on-Ouse wing leader had a nasty problem one day during this period. The wing ran into a jet stream returning home over the North Sea. The enormous headwinds meant that they were all critically short of fuel and it was impossible to keep the wing together. It became a matter of every man for himself and the aircraft landed all over the place. Miraculously they all landed safely.

One morning just after dawn, I was on quick reaction alert, sitting in my Meteor on the operational readiness platform at the end of runway 06. Ole Harve was my number two. It was snowing, visibility about 600 yards, cloud base about 200 ft. I was cold and the poor ground crew lads looked frozen. Suddenly over the telescramble line came the order, Scramble, Scramble. Engines were started, trolley-accs (mobile bettery packs) were disconnected and off we went in formation, climbing through cloud and snow so thick that Harve only just managed to stay in close formation. By the time we got to 35,000 ft or so, well out over the North Sea, the GCI radar controllers had lost the phantom blip, so we turned for home. Because of the very thick cloud and snow I decided that we would recover individually and Harve commenced his controlled descent first, for feed in to a GCA approach. I followed suit about two minutes later. As I was about to commence the GCA at 2,500 ft somewhere near Cambridge, my altimeter stuck, my airspeed indicator went to zero and the vertical speed indicator packed up, presumably the pitot head was frozen. Then all I could hear over the radio was a loud squealing noise, probably caused by ice on the aerial. This was not a good situation and the Martin Baker ejection seat came into consideration. However, there was a little time to spare so I motored back the canopy to help my vision and concentrated on maintaining an attitude on the artificial horizon that should give me a slow descent. The wheels and flaps were already down and I put on a touch of extra power. After a couple of minutes I could just make out some buildings below me so I flew level at about 150 ft and maintained course. I then tried the tower frequency on the radio. No good, so I kept on going straight ahead. Suddenly the squealing on the radio stopped and right below me was a piece of runway.

'Waterbeach Tower do you read?' I called.

'Affirmative, what is your position?' was the answer.

'I am just turning downwind,' I replied.

'Well we can't see you,' said the tower.

'I may be over Oakington, but wherever I am, I'm landing,' I said.

However, I missed the runway threshold on the first low circuit and commenced another. The weather was still awful, I had to stay down at about 150 ft above the ground and the instruments were still frozen up.

The second attempt was successful and to everybody's surprise, including mine, I had landed back on runway 06 at Waterbeach. Experience, instinct or pure luck?

We had another exciting and rather expensive day at Waterbeach. There were six of us up in the air from No. 56 Squadron when the weather started to deteriorate and we were ordered back to base. Harve was my number two again and the other two pairs were 'Hoppy' Hoppit, 'Pissy' Rimmington, Pete Martin and a pilot from Ceylon, Neil Weerasingh. I decided to let down over the sea with Harve and return at low level, maintaining visual contact with the ground and carry out the unofficial but highly effective, 'fish and duck' arrival. This entailed finding the Wash and King's Lynn, flying up the Great Ouse to Ely Cathedral and then up the river to the second tributary, at which was a big white pub called the Fish and Duck. Over the pub one turned onto 240 degrees magnetic and lowered the wheels. On crossing a railway line, full flap was selected and there straight ahead should be runway 24. We did this and landed successfully. Not so the other four.

The weather continued to deteriorate and then the problems started. The CRDF homer packed up and the four were diverted to Duxford for GCA radar approaches. They were now getting very short of fuel. For some reason none of them was able to land off their first approach. The first pair knew they were out of fuel and both pilots ejected safely. The other pair tried a second approach. The leader, I think it was Martin, flamed out at 800 ft and ejected safely. Neil Weerasingh flamed out very close to the ground and crashed into some trees close to the runway threshold. He was alive but rather badly hurt and I was later elected to break the news to his German wife. To my knowledge he never flew again.

Rimmington stood by a road with his parachute wrapped in his arms, thumbing a lift. A lorry stopped and he climbed aboard. The driver seemed remarkably unimpressed, so Rimmington said 'I've just baled out of an aircraft, you know.'

'Oh, aye,' said the lorry driver. 'I was at Arnhem meself. First Airborne Division'.

I later heard that Rimmington baled out of a Swift fighter reconnaissance plane in Germany. He found himself hanging upside down in his parachute and landed head first into the River Weser.

We had an exceptionally capable young sergeant pilot on No. 56 called Mike Warwick. I could never understand why he had not been commissioned. He was a nice lad and a very good aerobatic pilot. Alas, one day his Meteor broke up in the air during an aerobatic display and he was killed. We all went to London for the funeral and met his parents. It was a sad business, and this sort of thing was happening far too often. It was officially peace time but about one in ten pilots in Fighter Command was having an accident every year.

We took part in two enormous fly-pasts during 1953. One was the Coronation fly-past over Buckingham Palace and the other was the RAF Revue at Odiham. For the Coronation fly-past the RAF and RCAF squadrons in Fighter Command took part. We joined up in an enormous 'balbo' of vics of wings and it was very tricky to get this mass of aircraft joined up. On one of the rehearsals the Horsham St Faith wing leader, Bob Yule, was killed in a mid-air collision. His Meteor crashed into the middle of Woolwich Arsenal. The weather was poor on the actual day and the fly-past was done with the wings flying individually in line astern.This made the task much easier and safer.

One day No. 604 Auxiliary Squadron was operating from Waterbeach on an exercise. Their normal home was North Weald. We were watching them scramble when there was a bit of a bang followed by the familiar pall of oily black smoke. A figure came into view apparently unhurt – it was Norman Tebbit, then a BOAC first officer and a flying officer pilot on No. 604. The story was that he had abandoned take-off thinking his elevators were jammed. Apparently his elevator trim was set at full nose down.

I had my closest brush with death about this time. We were carrying out a series of simulated ground attacks on the army in the Thetford battle area. I had done one flight, and after refuelling went off again to take camera-gun pictures of tanks and trucks under camouflage netting – which looked exactly like tanks and trucks under netting. Some improvement needed there, I thought. As I pulled out of my first and, as it turned out, only attack, the aircraft mushed towards the ground at high speed. For about two seconds I was sure I was going to die as I rocketed between two trees at about 360 knots. I returned to base as the adrenalin dissipated from my system. It turned out that the ventral fuel tank had been mistakenly filled with fuel, which had naturally altered the flying characteristics of the aircraft. There was a faint smear of green on the bottom of the ventral tank.

'Well, Chief,' I said to the flight sergeant, 'I won't say anything if you don't'.

'Right you are, Sir,' said Chiefy.

Mind you, it must have impressed the hell out of the army.

Another friend of mine at Waterbeach was Joe Blyth, a flight commander on No. 63 Squadron who had recently returned from Korea. Joe, together with Max Scannell and one other chap had been with the Australian 77th Fighter Squadron, initially flying Mustangs. The squadron had re-equipped with Meteor 8s at Iwakuni in Japan and then returned to Korea. The Meteor was no match for the Mig-15, even if the pilots were better, and their main role was switched to ground attack. A friend from Rhodesia days, Jimmy Dolittle was shot down by ground fire and killed flying with the Australians.

Joe was an exceptional pilot and later commanded No. 8 Squadron during the Suez campaign. I heard that, flying his Venom in a series of attacks on a line of parked Migs, he just picked off one after another. The Egyptian flak gunners were all 'off duty' at the time. In eleven years after the Second World War, he was awarded two DFCs and two AFCs – quite an achievement in what was generally regarded as peace time.

During this period we had a goodwill visit from a squadron of Saab J29s of the Swedish air force. Some of our fighters were scrambled to meet them over the North Sea and escort them in to Waterbeach but there was a problem: they were too fast for us. Our Meteor 8s could not catch them – very embarrassing!

We had a squadron car on No. 56; an enormous Rolls-Royce Silver Ghost from the mid-1920s. One very foggy night, fourteen of us decided to visit Cambridge. Thirteen were accommodated inside and a lookout man was spreadeagled on the bonnet, clutching the flying lady. His job was to shout instructions to the driver. Unsurprisingly, the lookout man was 'Ole Harve'. After a somewhat perilous journey we parked outside the Baron of Beef and all piled out. It must have looked like a scene from a Marx Brothers movie. Meanwhile, the driver did a special trick with the ignition advance lever which caused a loud explosion in the exhaust pipe about thirty seconds after the engine had been switched off. A small crowd of bemused civilians looked on as we stood in line with our fingers in our ears. Then bang went the Rolls-Royce, and giving a loud cheer we all entered the pub.

So life went on at Waterbeach: air defence exercises, detachments to Wildenrath and Wunsdorf in Germany, air-to-air firing off the Farne Islands flying from Acklington in Northumberland.

Then I was sent off to the Central Fighter Establishment at West Raynham to do the instrument rating examiner's course. West Raynham was also the home of the Air Fighting Development Squadron (AFDS). Most of the pilots on that unit had been flying F-86s or F-84s with the Americans in

Korea, and they were impatiently awaiting the arrival of the first Hunters and Swifts for evaluation. A few weeks earlier I had played a bit of a trick on them. Paddy Barthrop had let me fly his personal Hawker Hurricane LF363. I pottered around East Anglia in the old machine, slightly alarmed by the amount of noise and vibration – it felt like something from the Flintstones era compared to a Meteor 8. To liven up my day I called up West Raynham on the radio and asked permission to do a low fly-past to show them a new aircraft. They excitedly agreed, thinking that at last a Hunter had arrived. They then asked me to delay a few minutes so that the pilots from AFDS could come to the control tower balcony for a better view. I then pottered slowly past the Control Tower in the Hurricane. The silence over the radio was deafening! Following a rather indifferent landing back at base I resigned myself to joining Harve on the orderly officer roster. However, nothing was said; Wing Commander Bird Wilson of AFDS obviously had a sense of humour.

The instrument rating examiner's course was quite demanding. For the final test, the pupil was strapped into the rear cockpit of a Meteor 7 that was totally blacked out. The instructor/examiner lined up on the runway, then the pupil carried out a take-off and climb, totally on instruments. Next came a fixed pattern exercise to test his accuracy in instrument flying. The instructor then did a couple of barrel rolls to topple the gyro of the artificial horizon, which left one with no attitude indicator apart from the rudimentary turn and slip instrument. Then one had to do tight turns at 60 degrees of bank, keeping within close limits of height and air speed. Finally, the instructor flamed out one engine and the pupil had to carry out a controlled descent followed by a GCA radar approach, at the end of which the instructor talked one into a blind landing. All this was done on one engine with no artificial horizon. I could not do it now to save my life.

Such were the standards required. The Meteor on one engine was in exactly the same situation as a Boeing 707 with two engines on the same side flamed out. The minimum control speeds were almost identical. Years later, an airline captain said to me, 'Of course I came up the hard way through civilian flying schools.' I could not decide whether to hit him or laugh.

A famous character based at West Raynham in this period was Wing Commander Binks, known as Binkie. He looked exactly like David Niven and he was always getting himself into trouble. His pyromaniacal tricks with lighter fuel had badly damaged two officers' mess bars. The story goes that he attended a reception in Kuala Lumpur and having ascended an impressive staircase, said to the splendid figure at the top, 'Hello Tosh, where's the bar?' The said splendid figure was General Sir Gerald Templar, a very able man, but not noted for his sense of humour.

On another occasion he was apparently called to the office of his AOC, Air Vice Marshal the Earl of Bandon. He was met by the personal assistant who told Binkie to be very contrite, as the AOC was really cross this time. The PA opened the door and announced, 'Sir, Wing Commander Binks.' Binkie apparently threw his hat through the door and entered the office on his knees. The Earl of Bandon had a notorious sense of humour, which I am sure saved Binkie. He later commanded 85 Squadron at West Malling. An extremely popular CO, his squadron was noted for its high morale.

The Earl of Bandon's final AOC's inspection before he moved on to greater things was done at Waterbeach. It was decided that it should be done in the morning and end with a formal lunch in the mess. After a minimum of parade-ground buffoonery and a fly-past where the squadrons formed the letters PB (whether that was supposed to stand for Paddy Bandon or Paddy Barthrop was never made clear), the inspection commenced. Apparently during his inspection of the WAAFs' quarters he pointed to a raised toilet seat and said to a flustered WAAF officer, 'Madam, how do you explain that?' The offending seat had been positioned that way earlier by his PA, of course.

The lunch was a bit of a riot and came after a session of rough shooting around the airfield. It ended with the AOC being driven from the mess in a landrover, firing his shotgun in the air. The driver, Flying Officer Plowman of No. 63 Squadron, appeared from where I was standing, to be stark naked. Somehow, I cannot imagine such a scene in the RAF today.

Then came big news. No. 56 Squadron was to be re-equipped with Swifts, making them the first swept-wing fighter squadron in the RAF. This did not turn out so well in the end, because the Swift was a bit of a dud. Its performance at high altitude was poor and No. 56 was eventually re-equipped with Hunters. However, the Swift gave a good account of itself later in the low-level fighter reconnaissance role.

As for me, I was posted to No. 111 Squadron, which was just re-forming at North Weald – Meteor 8s again. I pottered down to North Weald in the station Tiger Moth to say hello to everyone. It was a very foggy morning, so I followed the railway line down past Bishop's Stortford and landed on the grass in front of the control tower. 'You can't park 'ere,' said someone out of the gloom, so I taxied towards some hangars that were dimly visible through the mist. I made my mark with several of the station's dignitaries including the delightful station commander, Wing Commander Al Deere of Battle of Britain fame, and after lunch flew back to Waterbeach. Shortly thereafter I drove down to North Weald in my first motor car, a 1936 Morris 8 Open Tourer. It had cost me £85, it was red, it had the performance of a rice pudding and I loved it. My long love affair with cars had begun.

Gradually the pilots of the 'new' No. 111 Squadron arrived from all over: Germany, the Middle East and other Fighter Command squadrons. It was now Christmas 1953. During January we collected our aircraft – brand new, factory fresh Meteor 8s, with spring tab ailerons and the larger engine intakes. As Meteor day fighters went, they were the best and were probably among the last ever made. I spent a lot of time flying an Airspeed Oxford, ferrying our pilots to maintenance units to collect the new machines and by the end of January we were fully equipped and operational.

The CO was Harry Pears. Not the most erudite of men, his favourite adjective was 'fudging'. He never used a swear word just 'fudging this' and 'fudging that'. Unsurprisingly, he was nicknamed 'Fudger'. An innocent squadron wife, introduced to Squadron Leader Pears' wife at a cocktail party came out with a classic *faux pas*, when she said, 'Good Evening, Mrs Fudger.' One of our flight commanders was Jeff Jeffry. He had come from Germany and was always rushing about like the White Rabbit, ticking off items on his clipboard. The other flight commander was Bob Bingham, who never rushed anywhere.

Apart from Treble One, North Weald was home to two auxiliary squadrons, No. 601 and 604. No. 601 was the famous millionaire's outfit. It was run like a fashionable cavalry regiment; amongst its pilots was a White Russian prince and at least one 'Honorable'. It seemed that either a large income or impeccable social standing was a prerequisite for becoming a pilot in No. 601. They had red silk linings to their uniforms, and wore red socks and red bow ties with their mess kit – all a bit over the top, but they were a very competent squadron and well able to hold their own with the regulars. No. 604, which was of more plebeian cast was, at least during 1954, a hard-luck squadron. They had several accidents, including fatalities, most of which were sheer bad luck.

We were doing well on Treble One. Our serviceability was excellent with our brand new Meteors, and the average experience level of the pilots was high compared to that of most squadrons. It was during this period that I first met the famous air force padre, Father Joe McBraerty. We had a timed car race around the flower beds at the back of the North Weald officers' mess. It was soon decided that the circuit was a bit too short and, although it is difficult to believe now, we actually held up the traffic on the main road outside the front of the mess for a while to give us a longer lap. The race was won by Father Joe in, of all things, his Messerschmitt tandem-seat mini-car. Divine intervention perhaps!

Frequent events in those days were 'rat and terrier' exercises. Simulated low-level raiders would cross the coast and head inland. The Royal Observer Corps, still a going concern, would plot their position and course using a grid system and the positions were broadcast in a semi-continuous manner by the GCI station. The attacking aircraft were the rats. The terriers were pairs of fighters with the leader flying high at about 800 ft, listening to the radio broadcast, plotting the target's position and course and looking after the navigation. The number two, flying behind and below his leader at about 200 ft, was the lookout man. He would normally be the first to spot the target. It was much more exciting than practice interceptions at high altitude, but for those poor civilians in East Anglia and Lincolnshire the noise must have been horrendous; this was low flying with a vengeance. I once chased a Canadian F86 all the way across Norfolk until I finally got in a camera-gun shot as he climbed to clear some trees. Still, the Russians were coming – maybe.

About this time there were stories going around about the phantom dive of the Meteor 7 trainer. In certain conditions with wheels down and flaps extended, it was said to head down suddenly towards the ground of its own accord, but I did not really believe this. Then one day, 5 April 1954 I was giving a check ride to Flying Officer Johnny Hurll in the squadron Meteor 7. At the end of the detail we were turning finals on one engine (the other engine was throttled back, not flamed out thank heavens), when I noticed that we were yawing a bit and asked Johnny to keep his slip ball in the middle of the instrument. 'Right,' he said and then put in a big bootful of the wrong rudder. Down we went. 'I have control,' I shouted, opened up the throttle on the idling engine, banged in the correct rudder, and for a few seconds prayed. We recovered just above the trees. So that was the phantom dive. It seemed that the necessary ingredient was a lot of yaw. I never liked the fin and rudder set-up on the early Meteors. It did not even look right. The later design on the Meteor 8s and night fighters was much better.

About this time I decided that I really ought to get a driving licence. So off I went to Chigwell in my trusty Morris 8 to take the test. It seems strange now that one could fly high-performance fighters for years before owning a car, but in those days it was quite normal. I passed the test. At the same time one of our pilots, Pete Stowell, went for his test in his absolutely enormous Issota Frascini. Pete was quite a small chap and when he climbed into the driving seat, he practically disappeared. He was failed – almost certainly because the examiner was terrified.

On 24 September, I did an instrument flying check on Squadron Leader Butler from the handling squadron at Boscombe Down to renew his Green Card Instrument Rating. We were discussing the Hunter and he asked me if I would like to fly one. This was an opportunity not to be missed. On 27 September Eric Bennett and I flew down to Boscombe Down and there was this gorgeous-looking Hunter Mk 1. After a short briefing and cockpit familiarization, off I went.

This was normal procedure in those days; between the Mosquito and the Lightning I did not do one formal conversion course. The first thing I noticed was the firm suspension whilst taxiing; also, compared to the Meteor it was like a Ferrari after a Bentley. The performance was wonderful. As I climbed away over the Channel at 350 knots indicated, I saw four Meteors, probably from No. 1 Squadron at Tangmere, coming in from my left in a dummy attack but they simply couldn't catch me. At about 43,000 ft I pushed her into a shallow dive at full power and as we hit Mach 1, the only indication I felt was a very slight kick on the rudder pedals. Then it was back to Boscombe for a normal circuit and landing – wonderful. Little did I know that it was going to be years before I achieved Mach 1 again. Eric had a go next and was equally impressed, but we both decided that it was very short of fuel capacity. This was par for the course for any British fighter, but the Hunter 1 was particularly bad.

Eventually the inevitable happened on Treble One. Some aircraft were caught out by bad weather. Flying Officer Ginger Wright, diverting to Manston, realized he was not going to make it and tried to land on a road, wheels down, somewhere *en route*. This attempt was frustrated when a car pulled out of a side road so he raised the wheels and belly landed in a field. He was fine but the Meteor was rather bent.

On 25 September, about eight of us flew down to Filton, near Bristol to give army light flak gunners some fast, low-level targets to practise on in the South Wales area. We arrived just before lunch and that afternoon were due to carry out a sector reconnaissance to familiarize ourselves with the area. We declined beer but decided that a pint of cider would be quite acceptable. Oh dear. This was not the innocuous bottled cider, this was the genuine West Country scrumpy, probably stronger than white wine. We completed the exercise without incident, but the fact remains, we were all a bit the worse for wear. After landing I could not understand why my map was torn to shreds.

It was a big year for air defence exercises in 1954. One day the whole wing of three squadrons was scrambled, led by the wing leader, Jerry Gray. The unwieldy big wing was still in vogue; the spirit of Leigh Mallory and Bader lived on – quite ridiculous: any formation larger than a single squadron was just too clumsy. If a wing is operated as one large tactical formation, then any manoeuvring results in a complex aerial ballet as the separate 'finger fours' execute their cross-over turns and it becomes impossible to maintain a good look-out. Keeping the squadrons separated, though within mutually supporting ranges, improves flexibility and increases the chance of sighting a potential enemy. Fighter Command's close formation tactics in the early stages of the Battle of Britain resulted in a poor standard of look-out and consequently they were often bounced by the 'Hun in the sun'. Jerry Gray called out, 'Turning port go', then promptly turned right and ended up on his own. I found myself leading the whole North Weald Wing, but all went well after that. The exercise was completed and even the No. 601 princes declared themselves quite satisfied with my performance. Patronizing buggers, I thought to myself.

It was about time to say farewell to the Meteor. It was a reliable gentleman's machine, and the night fighter version with its long nose was a beautifully stable instrument flying platform. I never got more than 0.82 Mach number out of one before compressibility set in and control was lost, but I am sure that those of us who were around at the time never forgot the spine-tingling sound of a Meteor wing at high speed, running in for a break-and-stream landing. We called it the blue note and it was quite unique.

In January 1955 we were at Acklington in Northumberland for air-to-air firing practice. I think we spent as much time shovelling snow as flying on that detachment. Roger Topp arrived at that time to take over the squadron from Harry Pears. One snow-bound evening we were playing a typically silly fighter pilots' game. It was a race that involved climbing up into the ceiling through a trapdoor, traversing the building on the ceiling beams and reappearing in the bar through another man-hole. During the course of the game the Acklington station commander entered the bar and engaged me in polite conversation. Suddenly there was a loud noise from overhead and a shower of plaster and splintered wood, and down through the ceiling came Flying Officer 'Tatty' Shields. He landed at the feet of the station commander, who was, as P.G. Wodehouse would put it, 'not completely gruntled'. That was the end of the game and it cost us all a couple of pounds or so for repairs to the ceiling.

The Treble One pilots were all big fans of the *Goon Show*. Silence had to be observed in the mess anteroom as we listened to the surreal and ludicrous antics of Neddie Seegoon, Gryp Pipe Thynne etc. Eric Bennett began to talk almost permanently like Bluebottle. I believe this enthusiasm for the Goons extended throughout Fighter Command.

Then a signal arrived. 'Flight Lieutenant Mercer to report to HQ Far East Air Force, Changi, Singapore, for flight commander duties. To arrive Changi three weeks from today.' Good grief, I thought. Treble One were expecting to get Hunters soon, No. 43 Squadron already had them, and I was being sent to the ends of the earth to fly bloody Vampires. I had flown a Vampire 5 once: a pleasant little machine with an engine that reminded one of a vacuum cleaner and, I recalled that compressibility problems started at about Mach 0.78. So it was farewell to Eric Bennett, Dave Goodwin, George Aird, Dave Garrett, Dickie Lord and the others. The arrival of Roger Topp promised a more dynamic leadership style for Treble One.

I disposed of my 1936 Aston Martin, for which I had traded in my Morris, to Jack Bond, a London classic car dealer. I then collected my kit and proceeded to Lynham where I climbed aboard a Hastings of Transport Command. Five days later we landed at Changi having stopped at Castle Idris, Libya, Habbanya, Iraq, Karachi, Pakistan, and Negombo, Ceylon, *en route*. The captain let me have a brief go at the controls over the Indian Ocean. They felt ludicrously heavy to me and I wondered how on earth the pilots managed to land something so unresponsive. Changi felt decidedly hot after the Northumberland winter.

CHAPTER SIX

Fighter Bombers

I was warmly received at Tengah, where I was now a flight commander on No. 60 Squadron, another squadron with an impressive war record. I took over from Pat Hannafin. The other flight commander was Terry Kearns, a Kiwi and a very highly decorated former No. 617 (Dambuster) Squadron pilot. The CO was Hugh Webb, a nice man, but I never saw him fly an aircraft. Also at Tengah was No.1(B) Squadron RAAF with Lincolns and No. 45 Squadron with Hornets. Another fighter squadron, No. 14(F) Squadron RNZAF were due to arrive soon, and all this promised a lively mess life. On my first night the boys took me out to Fatties in Albert Street, Singapore and I fell for the usual trick: 'Have the green chillies Brian – they're not a bit hot.'

The Malayan Emergency was still goingstrong at this time and there was a big security flap on. A 1,000 lb bomb had vanished from the bomb dump and everyone had visions of the Raffles Hotel being blown up. However, when the perpetrators were subsequently found trying to saw the bomb open, they turned out not to be communist terrorists after all, but Chinese lads after explosives to make fireworks. After that security was tightened up at the Tengah bomb dump.

One always felt at a disadvantage on arrival at a tropical base. New boys cut a faintly ridiculous figure, with their brand new khaki drill and white knees. I was no exception, but it did not take me long to refit with much superior, locally made tropical uniform and quite soon my knees were as brown as everyone else's. No. 60 Squadron's pilots were a lively and rather raffish collection of aviators. Their idea of a good jape was to have a race to the Equator and back. The fact that the Equator was in Indonesia didn't seem to bother them at all. They also never seemed to fly above 20,000 ft. 'Much too tedious, old chap, to climb higher' was the attitude. On an early flight, when I was still acquainting myself properly with the Vampire, I flew as number two to Jimmy Hanson to fire some rockets at China Rock just off the south-east coast of Malaya. He led me back south of Singapore island, flying so low that Chinese fishermen were jumping out of their sampans into the sea to avoid fatal contact with Jimmy's Vampire. Well, this is certainly different I thought to myself. It was not long before I had them up at 40,000 ft for their battle formation drill and further trips to the Equator were out. Potentially lethal straffing runs over Chinese sampans were also discouraged.

Wing Commander Marcus Knight had been replaced as Wing Commander Flying by Joe Holmes, who had achieved some fame in Germany, I believe at Fassberg, when he found himself in charge of a parade. The padre had not turned up for prayers, and Joe uttered the immortal words: 'Right men, let's have two verses of "Holy Holy" and then bugger off.' This sort of thing was bound to endear him to the Australians. Terry Kearns was a lovely chap, if a bit wild. He was fond of driving a Landrover up the steps into the mess anteroom and he was possibly still slightly 'flak happy' from his wartime days on No. 617 Squadron.

I was about to have a go in one of No. 45 Squadron's Hornets, and was looking forward to this as the Hornet was one of the really great piston-engined aircraft. It was like a faster Mosquito with the vices removed. The props turned different ways removing the tendency to swing, and the undercarriage was quicker-acting and much less bulky. Alas, it never happened. Some government inspectors turned up to inspect the Hornets and were pretty horrified at the deterioration induced by the tropical climate. The result was that all three Hornet squadrons in the Far East were grounded: No. 80 at Kai Tak, Hong Kong, No. 33 at Butterworth, Malaya, and of course No. 45. So I never got to fly a Hornet. No. 45 re-equipped with Venoms and moved up to Butterworth. They later became a Canberra light bomber squadron. No. 33 disbanded and later re-formed as a night fighter squadron in England, and No. 80 simply vanished into the pages of history.

In addition to our air defence role, our main job in Malaya was to carry out 'Firedog' operations against the communist terrorists. I myself did about fifty, but during the two and a half years I was out there, I knew of only two occasions when we actually hit any terrorists with our cannons, rockets or bombs. If you could not see your target then you were mostly wasting your time, and the targets were largely invisible in the Malayan jungle, hidden by the lush canopies of close-packed and very large trees.

The biggest success was Operation Kingly Pile in 1956. The army had captured a communist and he was able to tell us where and when the Johore Company of the Malayan Races Liberation Army was meeting. They were wiped out in a closely co-ordinated raid by two fighter bomber squadrons, a Canberra squadron and the Australian Lincolns. As a result, Johore State became a safe area. However, most of the time all we did was blast holes in the jungle, which I suspect is what the Americans mostly did later in Vietnam with their B-52 raids.

Life was good at Tengah. We got on very well with the Aussies with very few exceptions; there were just a couple of professional Pommie haters. The Kiwis arrived, so we now had two fighter squadrons again after the departure of No. 45. The New Zealanders would go for a month or so as quiet as monks in a monastery, then *boom*; there would be hakas, songs, vast quantities of beer and general mayhem. This would then be followed by another quiet period. We and the Australians had a rather more measured approach to social drinking – pretty constant but less frenetic. The engineer officer of the Australian squadron was called 'Uncle Jim'. A tall, laconic figure in the regulation slouch hat, he would occasionally get a little inebriated at the bar and then he would launch into a song from the Second World War. It was sung to the tune of the 'Battle Hymn of the Republic' and went as follows:

First Verse: The starting of the Beaufort is a most peculiar art.

No matter how you prime it, the bastard will not start.

In fact on some occasions when the dew is on the grass

You might as well stick the priming pump up Pratt and Whitney's arse.

Chorus: CO CI everybody come,

Come and see the Beaufort boys sitting on their bum

Trying to start their Beauforts amidst the mightly roar

From all the Lockheed Hudsons that have taken off before.

2nd Verse: Enthusiastic fitters and some pilots on the course

Have found to their intense dismay and sometimes their remorse

To overprime the Beaufort is a wilful misdemeanour

And has about the same effect as a badly aimed *eneema*.

For maximum effect the song has to be sung in a broad Australian accent.

Another Aussie character was Flying Officer Dalton. He greeted everyone, irrespective of rank, race or creed, with the words, 'G'Day, squire,' He was, of course, known as Squire Dalton. Another Australian pilot called Ken Dee had an impressive trick. He would appear over the runway threshold in his big silver Lincoln at quite high speed, crank on a lot of bank and do a 360 degree turn at low level whilst extending wheels and flaps, then touch down for landing, all in fifty seconds.

About two months after my arrival at Tengah our Venoms started to arrive. It was a much more effective weapon than either the Meteor or the Vampire. It was faster, it could fly much higher, it had a longer range and a better rate of climb, and it was a good gun platform. No more worrying take-offs on hot afternoons in a Vampire with two 500 lb bombs slung under the wings. The Venom, with two 1,000 lb bombs took off like a homesick angel by comparison, though I felt some concern the first time I did this. As I approached the aircraft from the front, the bombs looked almost as big as the fuselage.

We now had a new squadron commander, Pete Lovell. He had commanded a Kittyhawk squadron in North Africa during the war. He had a dry sense of humour and was an able administrator, but as far as flying was concerned, he had gone off the boil so to speak. He rarely flew, and when he did he was not very safe. A strange thing about flying, particularly fighter flying, if you stop for a while you very quickly lose your edge and if you stop for long enough, you can become apprehensive about starting again. It did not really matter to me, as he left the operational side largely in my care.

Terry Kearns left and was replaced by Derek Yates from one of the Linton-on-Ouse Sabre squadrons. We made No. 60 Squadron into a pretty good fighting unit. Our gunnery scores were good and tactical battle formation exercises were now done up at 45,000–48,000 ft. The principle that the high man controls the battle had not changed since Von Richthofen.

Frank Grimshaw arrived from a Church Fenton squadron and a new pilot, John Pusey, arrived from England. Frank had completed the Fighter Weapons School Course and was our pilot attack instructor (PAI). The high altitude flying we were now doing led to an amusing article in the *Straits Times*. For the first time condensation trails were appearing in the skies over Singapore and the paper started speculating about the arrival of UFOs. I got a Venom up to 54,000 ft one morning. This was possible because of the high tropopause and the resulting very cold temperature at altitude. The Venom was still climbing, albeit very slowly, but despite my pressure waistcoat, common sense dictated that I should descend.

Some weeks later I had a canopy shatter at about 35,000 ft. There was a big bang and a cloud of dust, and I thought the engine had blown up. It was the sudden decompression of course. The truth dawned as I started to feel very, very cold; the temperature would have been in the region of −50 degrees celsius. Throttle closed, full dive brakes, half roll and down I went before I froze to death. I do not care for tropical heat normally, but I was very happy to find it that day.

In October 1955, Pete Lovell let me start a small aerobatic team of four Venoms. John Pusey, David Ryles and Bob Johnson were keen to have a go, so we did the occasional practice flight and eventually achieved a reasonable standard.

On 15 February 1956 the aerobatic team got its chance and we flew up to Bangkok for a display on the 16th. The Americans were there in strength and were to do a massed parachute drop as part of the display.

We were put up in a very ordinary hotel; and a fellow guest was an American 'exotic dancer' called Miss Jenny Lee, the

Bazoom Girl. She was rather nice but her manager looked a bit of a thug and we suspected that he occasionally knocked her about a little. We caught her act, the highlight of which was the contra rotating of tassels attached to her nipples. I have never understood how that worked.

At the briefing for the display a delay was announced while we waited for Colonel Pritchard, who had brought some F-84s across from Clark Field in the Philippines. Eventually he walked in, followed by his pilots. They all had identical crewcuts and, being *Goon Show* fans, we immediately christened them the Hairy Bald Headhunters (I know that makes little sense but neither does the *Goon Show*). When he learned we were to do a formation aerobatic display, Colonel Pritchard decided they could do the same without any practice or training. That was very nearly a lethal decision. Halfway through a roll during their display, they experienced a situation that we later called the 'dishing effect'. This is when the wing men get into a position where they are both banking towards the leader, almost certainly caused by the leader changing his rate of roll in the middle of the manoeuvre. It was the nearest thing to a mid-air collision without one actually occurring that I ever saw.

Our display went as planned, enlivened by a Thai air force Grumman Bearcat which managed to land downwind with its wheels retracted amid a shower of sparks. I never found out why. The massed paratrooper drop produced a moment of real drama. One of the soldiers' parachute 'candled' and as he dropped through his colleagues on his way to certain death, one of them grabbed his collapsed chute and they both reached the ground safely.

Following a round of cocktail parties that evening, we had a race against the American Marines in motorized rickshaws, I cannot remember who won.

Back at base on the 17 February, we looked forward to Exercise Welcome, the arrival of the two Royal Navy aircraft carriers, *Albion* and *Centaur*, and the experience of dogfighting against the Navy Sea Hawks. On 8 March I took a flight of Venoms up to Kuala Lumpur. The carriers were due off the Malayan coast next morning and planned a dawn strike on Kuala Lumpur. We were tasked to intercept them. The incoming Sea Hawks were picked up by the coastal radar and we were scrambled just as dawn was breaking. There ensued a most splendid dogfight over and around Kuala Lumpur in the misty early morning. We flew four sorties that day, finally landing back at Tengah as the carriers steamed down the Malacca Straits.

A couple of Sea Hawk squadrons landed at Tengah and were based there for a while. That livened up the mess even more. One of the squadron commanders was Lieutenant Commander Dickie Reynolds, about whom it was said that he had astounded the Americans one day by looping a Sea Hornet with both propellers feathered. In exchange for a flight in a Venom, he let me have a go in one of his Sea Hawks; the only thing I knew about it was that 110 knots 'over the hedge' was about right for landing. A petty officer showed me around the cockpit and described how to start the engine. He also pointed to a red light and said, 'If that light comes on, don't 'ang about, sir, eject immediately.' Apparently it was a fire warning light for a fuselage fuel tank. The navy had suffered a horrific accident on their way out to the Far East. It seems that at the very moment the button for the catapult launch was pressed, a Sea Hawk burst into flames and the poor pilot was launched off in a ball of fire.

Having started the engine I was about to taxi when I realized that the wings were still folded. The Petty Officer returned and showed me what to do, and off I went. It was a nice machine, pretty and strong like all Sydney Camm designs but I felt it was a bit underpowered for its weight. The single-seat Venom definitely had the edge in rate of climb and manoeuvrability and generally felt lighter, if a little more crude. I managed to get a few good camera-gun shots of the navy, one over the Johore Straits as I rocketed past a moored Sunderland flying boat and another as I chased a Sea Hawk between two Tengah hangars. We were a spirited lot in those days.

We had a party aboard *Centaur* one evening and of course some clown pinched a ceremonial cannon from the quarterdeck. The navy was not amused and the said cannon was returned. Finally the Navy departed and life at Tengah returned to more or less normal.

In 1956 England won the ashes. There was, of course, a big celebration party in the bar. Frank Grimshaw and I were playing a duet on the piano and an Australian (I suspect Squire Dalton), threw a whole bunch of firecrackers into the body of the piano. The resulting explosion was quite spectacular. Frank and I tried to continue with our black faces and singed eyebrows but it was no good, half the notes did not work. The piano was a total wreck. I think that was the night the medical officer had to be carried to bed. Normally a quiet man, he had started throwing bottles at the ceiling fan. This potentially lethal activity had to be stopped and he was carried away protesting.

Pete Lovell left and Squadron Leader Alan Jenkins arrived from AFDS. He had done a flying tour with the Americans on F-86s in Korea, so now we had a proper flying squadron commander. David Ryles left and Alan Jenkins said he would fly as my number three in the aerobatic team. Not many squadron commanders would have done that; he was a very nice man. Derek Yates went back to the UK for compassionate reasons and was replaced by Bob Price from FEAF HQ and he later took over the number four position from Bob Johnson in the aerobatic team.

One lunchtime, who should walk into the mess bar, but Father Joe McBraerty.

'Hello, boys,' he called out, 'let's all have a little drink.'

This was greeted by a chorus of 'Sorry, Father, I've got to fly', or 'I'm playing tennis in ten minutes', or 'I have to meet my wife', to which Father Joe replied 'Ah, what's the matter with you; you're behaving like a lot of Protestants.'

At a dining-in night in the mess, a farewell speech was made by Pete Breslain, a No. 60 Squadron pilot who was returning home. During the speech he told the following joke.

'One night three airmen were walking back from Tengah village: An Englishman, an Australian and a New Zealander [chorus of jeers and cheers from the assembled throng]. Suddenly, in the moonlight they saw the rear end of a pig struggling to get through a fence.

'I wish that was Marilyn Monroe,' said the Englishman.

'I wish it was Jayne Mansfield,' said the Australian.

'The New Zealander said, "I wish it was dark!"'

There were gales of laughter and a chorus of jeers from the New Zealanders. Father Joe was having a good chuckle. The Church of England padre however, strode from the dining room wearing a very sour expression.

The RAF had been invited to participate in the celebrations for the first anniversary of South Vietnam's independence, and it was decided to send our aerobatic team up to Saigon to give a display. On 23 October 1956, I took six Venoms up to Butterworth on the north-west coast of Malaya, which was later to become the fighter base for the RAAF in that part of the world, and which was the scene of an amusing incident.

The group captain station commander, a rather stern and forbidding figure, had a pet monkey, which was detested by all the station staff as it had a habit of wandering into offices and creating havoc with any paperwork lying about. One evening, a group of young fighter pilots was playing a rather raucous game in the mess billiard room. In the course of the game, a billiard ball went sailing through the air and flew out of a window. The group captain was walking past outside with his monkey on his shoulder. The billiard ball struck the Group Captain on the head and he cried out. The monkey became frightened and bit a large chunk out of his master's ear. The result of all this was no more monkey, a group captain with a bandaged head and a group of very pleased admin. officers. The said fighter pilots were very popular, except with the monkey.

After a night stop at Butterworth, we flew in loose battle formation to Tan Son Knut Airport, Saigon. Years later I was to become well acquainted with this airfield under very different circumstances at the height of the Vietnam War.

1956 however was for Vietnam between wars, but the French disaster at Dien Bien Phu was still fresh in the mind and the number of bullet-scarred buildings was ominous. There was still some French military presence and a number of Americans of the military advisory groups. A couple of my pilots had drinks with the French Foreign Legion one evening, a number of the legionnaires were ex-Waffen SS! Together with two pilots, I stayed with the British Charge D'Affaires, Mr Etherington Smith. The others stayed with the Air Attaché, Wing Commander Bill Mills, a former commander of No. 60 Squadron. Our ground crew flew up in a Bristol Freighter of the RNZAF.

On 25 October four of us took off to do some aerobatic practice and familiarize ourselves with the local area. The following day there was a big fly-past over Saigon, mostly of US Navy planes of the Seventh Fleet with us tagging along. That night there was a tremendous round of cocktail parties and receptions. At this time the South East Asia Treaty Organization (SEATO) was still going strong, and there were diplomats and their ladies, and senior officers of many countries, all decked out in white and gold uniforms. We looked quite good too in our white tropical mess kit and it was all great fun but not particularly good preparation for the following day's aerobatic display.

The main street of Saigon was, in those days, the Rue Cattinat, a typically wide Parisian-style boulevard which ran in a straight line from the Saigon River to a palace-like building at the far end. President Diem of South Vietnam was to watch our display from the bridge of an Australian destroyer, HMAS *Anzac*, moored in the river at the beginning of the street. Next to *Anzac* was the American cruiser *Los Angeles*.

The four of us took off and performed our routine of loops, rolls and steep wing-overs in tight formation, finishing off with a bomb-burst manoeuvre right over *Anzac*. My line of departure was straight up the Rue Cattinat below the level of the buildings. I can still see thousands of light brown faces and big eyes rushing past underneath at about 400 mph. A few minutes later we landed back at Tan Son Knut, hot and sweaty. Alan Jenkins was leaning against his wing, looking a bit pale and wondering if he should be sick – too many cocktails and curried prawns the night before, I expect. Before we could leave to get changed, a Vietnamese officer ran up to us and said, 'President Diem liked your display so much he would like you to do it again!'

'What now?' I asked.

'Yes,' was the reply.

Alan groaned but went off to have a shower. As soon as the planes were refuelled, off we went again and repeated the display. Oddly enough, Alan felt much better after the second show.

That evening there were more cocktail parties and the whole jolly crowd ended up aboard *Los Angeles*. What the majority had forgotten was that US Navy ships are 'dry' and it was not long before there was a mass exodus; the head of the line of people was ascending the gangway of *Anzac* as the tail descended that of *Los Angeles*. Commander Peel and his Australian crew did us proud and the mainbrace was thoroughly spliced. However, I heard that the next morning when *Anzac* departed, someone forgot to cast off one cable and the ship gracefully eased out into the Saigon River, towing behind a large section of wooden jetty.

At one of the cocktail parties, a senior American officer was heard to remark, 'We move the whole Seventh Fleet, deploy hundreds of airplanes, spend millions, and the RAF comes up here with a few Mickey Mouse fighters and steals the show.' We enjoyed that.

One evening as we were enjoying some quiet beers, a Frenchman ran into the bar waving a newspaper. The Suez campaign had just started. We immediately began discussing the best route and staging posts for our deployment to the Middle East. It was not to be, of course – John Foster Dulles saw to that. There were some awkward moments between the Royal Navy and the US Sixth Fleet in the eastern Mediterranean and we had to give up. President Eisenhower went back to the golf course and Anthony Eden resigned.

The next morning we set off to fly direct to Singapore. About 100 miles out over the South China Sea, my number two, Flying Officer Mick Mercer (no relation), called out in an understandably high-pitched voice, 'Leader, my fire warning light has come on.' The other four planes carried on to Singapore whilst I turned back to Saigon with my number two. I inspected his aircraft closely for any signs of smoke or fire, but there was no indication of trouble so we descended back to Saigon at reduced power. It turned out to be a false alarm, but it took days to fix.

In the meantime we returned to Singapore in the venerable Bristol Freighter to find a bit of trouble going on. At this time Singapore and Malaya were approaching independence and the local politicians were jockeying for position, so there was a riot. As usual with these affairs, the 'rogues from the bazaar' joined in, hoping for some loot. A number of air force officers from Tengah manned the barricades in company with Tommies and Gurkhas. Deployments in aid of the civil power were pretty routine in those dying days of the British Empire. Eventually I got back to Saigon and flew the repaired Venom back home on 1 November.

The weather over Malaya could be really horrible. The biggest cumulonimbus clouds in the world grow there. I was leading four Venoms in a climb through layer cloud one morning when we accidentally found a cumulonimbus hiding in the layers. The close formation broke up at once in the turbulence and the rain was so heavy that two of the pilots' engines flamed out. Luckily both were able to relight.

One night six of us did a cross-country flight up to Khota-Bahru over Penang and Kuala Lumpur and then back to Tengah. We went off at about four minute intervals. The weather was beautiful until we reached the Kuala Lumpur area, where there was a mass of storm clouds which seemed to stretch for ever both left and right. I went through at 48,000 ft and the turbulence was frightful, only the artificial horizon was any use. Frank Grimshaw climbed to over 50,000 ft and was still in it. Bob Johnson got into a spin at over 40,000 ft and did not recover until 15,000 ft. I landed first and anxiously counted the returning Venoms. All returned and six chastened pilots repaired to the mess bar. As we entered, a big fat Australian started up. 'Here come the Poms. They're all yellow-bellies, Poms.' He had picked the wrong moment; I was so incensed that he ended up on the floor. His fellow

Australians who were present, all No. 1 (B) Squadron aircrew, were on my side.

The Venom Mk 1 was fine up to about Mach 0.85, when compressibility set in with a vengeance. Then down went one wing and down went the Venom. Recovery took several thousand feet. The Mk 4, which we got later, was quite a bit better as it had powered ailerons. I once got one up to Mach 0.91 with the wings still more or less level but the elevator control at that speed was non-existent.

Dive bombing could be a problem. Often the cloud base was too low, particularly in the afternoons as the dreaded cumulonimbus started to build up. I remember once having to lob 1,000 lb bombs into a hillside at the end of a valley, then having to pull like hell to get away from the bomb blast. Another factor was the strain that dive bombing put on the aircraft structure; after about 750 hours of fighter-bomber work, the Venom airframe was reaching the end of its life. We developed a technique of level bombing using the reflection of the gun-sight ring in the sunshield of the sight to get an aiming datum. We adjusted the sunshield until the reflection of the sight ring just rested on the aircraft's nose, then played with different heights and air speeds until we could achieve reasonable accuracy. But it was all pretty Heath Robinson stuff.

Then FEAF got a clever bit of kit called a forward radar control post. With that we could level bomb with reasonable accuracy even at night. FEAF HQ said that single-engined day fighters could not formate at night, but they were wrong! There is no problem flying formation at night. The only tricky bit is joining up together in the first place. To prove the point, one night I led twelve Venoms in close formation, navigation lights on, in a series of fly-pasts over Changi and Fairy Point FEAF headquarters. The response was complete silence.

A regular event was a visit by a flight of American B-29s from Okinawa. These visits were called Exercise Joss Stick. We did bomber affiliation work with them and at the end of the visit there was a big party in the mess garden, after which we had a show of all the camera-gun films from the exercise. The bomber crews found the films rather sobering. They seemed to show that nothing had changed since the Second World War and unescorted bombers in daylight were dead meat against fighters – echoes of Schweinfurt and Regensberg.

The Australians were paid more than us. We had the occasional rather stormy mess meeting as they voted for extra messing to improve the food. The problem was that their governments paid the bill for them; ours, unsurprisingly, did not.

In the time of Pete Lovell, there was an AOC's inspection and as my squadron commander had conveniently sprained his ankle, I found myself stamping about, waving a sword in front of the troops, which always made me feel faintly ridiculous. The AOC at the time was 'Digger' Kyle, an Australian serving in the RAF. The Aussies were drawn up on parade just behind us, looking most unhappy. The AOC was a bit late and it was very hot. Suddenly a loud Aussie voice called out 'Hey Hughie, what time's the old bugger supposed to get 'ere?' A titter ran through our ranks, as the saying goes. Suppressing a grin and assuming my fiercest parade-ground expression, I swivelled around and called, 'Silence in the ranks.' No one was fooled.

Apart from one horrid incident in 1955, No. 60 Squadron had a reasonable run as far as accidents were concerned, and that incident was caused by no more than an electrical short. An unfortunate armourer was plugging in the electrical 'pig tails' on the rockets of an aircraft at the end of the runway when a rocket went off. The poor chap was right behind the rocket motor at the time and the devastating effects can be imagined. We did, however, have a spate of jammed undercarriages and collapsed nosewheels, I wonder if the enormous changes in environment to which the aircraft were subjected was a significant factor. Our aircraft were parked in the sun, and the shade temperature was often 32 degrees celsius. Twenty minutes later the aircraft could be up at 48,000 ft where the temperature might be as low as –63 degrees, which must have had some effect on the mechanical systems and their designed clearances.

One night the Australians had a real drama. Six Lincolns loaded with about fourteen 1,000 lb bombs each, departed in a stream take-off for a night bandit strike. To the north of Tengah, across the Johore Straits, is a big pimple of a hill. The departure track had been plotted to pass right over it, but somebody had got their sums wrong. Five Lincolns cleared the hill, but one did not. It smashed through the trees on the top of the hill and branches and foliage came into the cockpit through the broken windscreen. The captain was injured, but somehow the aircraft kept flying. Joe Holmes was on board and he dragged the injured pilot out of the seat. With two engines out of action, they turned west towards the coast, jettisoning the bombs, and ditched in the Malacca Straits just off the coast. They all survived, which was a minor miracle.

The Wing Commander Tech at Tengah, displaying a very black sense of humour, poked his head through the door where the Board of Inquiry was assembled. 'Why don't you say it was a bird strike?' he said. 'Mind you, you would have to say the bird was in its nest at the time.' I believe the Australians were not amused.

No. 14 (F) Squadron had been having a somewhat torrid time. One pilot belly landed on a beach following an engine failure. Another, turning finals in his Venom, was so fascinated by a fire that had broken out in his squadron dispersal that he forgot to lower his wheels. Another got into a spin near Batu Pahat and, failing to recover, had ejected safely; he had possibly been holding in some 'out spin' aileron. Then, following an engine failure on take-off, a young chap had crashed into a village just south of the airfield. Alan Jenkins and I witnessed this one and rushed towards the accident in the squadron Landrover. We met the young Kiwi calmly walking towards us, quite unhurt. It had been a bad run for No. 14, but nobody was killed or even badly injured.

I had a fright one morning. Climbing through 30,000 ft somewhere near Kluang, there was a very loud bang, followed by an extremely strong smell of fuel in the cockpit and the engine started to surge. Closing the throttle, I turned back towards Tengah. When I was close to the airfield, I cut the engine off completely and did a dead-stick landing on the runway.

It was now the turn of No. 60 Squadron to suffer misfortune. One night I was leading four pairs of Venoms. My number two was young Billy Alcock. Halfway down the runway he called out, 'Abandoning take-off.' He had heard a bang and his aircraft had swung to the right. He brought it to a halt just short of the bomb dump. Meanwhile as I was circling the airfield, I heard the tower instructing the other aircraft to return to dispersal, then they told me to divert to Changi. It was not long before I learned what had happened. Two airmen who worked in the control tower had taken an open Landrover to lay two glim lamps on one of the taxi tracks. It was later discovered that they had actually laid them on the edge of the runway, having driven past a red traffic light to get there. They had parked the Landrover right on the runway edge and Billy's right wing, just inboard of the tip tank, had decapitated both of them. Still unaware of what had happened, he was being driven back from his immobile aircraft when in the headlights of the vehicle he saw the MO picking up a human head. By the time I got back from Changi and went to the mess, the other pilots had got him fairly relaxed again by feeding him brandy. None of it was in any way his fault of course.

That was bad enough but it was about to get worse, much worse. A nice young pilot, Flying Officer Lincoln, naturally nicknamed Abe, had joined the squadron. I did a dual-check ride on him on 25 May 1957 and rated him as high average. Two weeks later, he was dead. I was sitting in a first-floor office as a member of a Board of Inquiry with a squadron leader from FEAF HQ and a New Zealand pilot from No. 14 (F) Squadron. Suddenly the Kiwi pilot called out, 'Christ, there goes another one.' There was a loud crump and the New Zealander went as white as a sheet. I rushed to the window and saw smoke and flames coming from the area of the married quarters. A sergeant ran out of an office below and I heard him call out, 'Oh God, that looks like my house.' It was. Young Abe Lincoln was taking off in formation with Alan Jenkins. Immediately after becoming airborne, his aircraft slewed to the right in a gentle bank and ploughed into the married quarters. He was killed, as were two wives and a child. To make matters worse, the local fire engine coming to help crashed outside the camp gates and there were more casualties. A pall of gloom settled over Tengah.

The Board of Inquiry arrived headed by the same group captain who had given my navigator and myself such a miserable welcome to West Malling seven years earlier. Everyone was thoroughly grilled, and he thought he had me as I talked about the use of one- third flap for take-off. 'Ah, but the flaps on the Venom 1 go further down than the flaps on the Venom 4, so one-third flap is different on the two types,' he said. 'Yes, but the flap area is bigger on the Venom 4, so that cancels out the difference,' I replied. What really happened? No one will ever be sure but the most likely explanation is that young Abe got a bit below his leader after lift-off and probably jerked the stick back; not a good thing to do on a Venom at slow speed. I think he stalled the aircraft.

A big safety drive had started throughout the RAF about this time. No one could argue with that, because far too many young men had been killed over the past decade. However, gloom is not allowed to persist on fighter squadrons and very soon things got back to normal. It was now almost time for me to return home. Clive Francis arrived to take over from me, in funny khaki drill and with white knees.

What was going to happen to me? The dreaded Duncan Sandy's 1957 Defence White Paper had struck. Big, ugly missiles were the thing now and aeroplanes were out. What about the Harriers in the Falklands twenty-five years later and the Tornados in the Gulf and over the Balkans, more than thirty years later? White-faced station commanders were assembling their men in station cinemas and telling them that their squadrons were disbanded, with immediate effect. The RAF fighter units were decimated. All the auxiliary squadrons were scrapped and the navy was soon to lose its aircraft carriers. How many lives would have been saved in the Falklands if we had been able to position a proper fleet carrier out there with interceptor fighters and long-range radar to give us decent early warning?

The Earl of Bandon later arrived as the new commander of the FEAF. He and I always seemed to follow each other around the air force. He opened a new swimming pool at the Changi Officers' Club. 'Ladies and gentlemen,' he said, 'I declare this swimming pool open.' He then stepped into the deep end in full uniform, leaving just his hat floating on the surface. We all loved him.

CHAPTER SEVEN

No. 111 Squadron and the Black Arrows

After a long flog back to England in a chartered Hermes, I reported to the Ministry in Whitehall to learn my fate. There I met Squadron Leader Pete Latham, who was in charge of aircrew postings.

'How would you like to go back to Treble One as a flight commander?' he said. I could not believe my luck. 'First, though, you had better do the day fighter leaders' course.' This is getting better and better I thought. After a heartfelt 'Thank you', I went off on leave.

A nice letter arrived from Air Vice Marshal Hancock, the AOC in Malaya, to say I had been Mentioned in Dispatches.

In October 1957 I arrived at West Raynham for the DFL course. Scott Vos, my old CO from No. 56 Squadron, was in charge of the unit. Eric Bennett from Treble One and Dickie Wirdnam from Waterbeach were on the staff, so it was like 'Old Home Week' as the Americans say. The unit was equipped with the Hunter Mk 6, the first really good Hunter. It had the extra fuel capacity that first arrived on the Mk 4 and the engine surging and gun-firing problems had been solved. It had 3,000 lb more thrust and a saw tooth on the wing leading edge to cure the high altitude/high Mach number pitch-up problem. That last problem could be quite nasty. My friend Doug Dalleson, the well known Kiwi extrovert, told me what happened to him one day. He was in a simulated dogfight at high altitude. In a hard turn, his Hunter suddenly tucked into the turn. He said one of his eyeballs came out of its socket and he had to land his Hunter holding the eyeball in his hand. The 'stringy bits' were still connected and the doctors were able to stuff it back in. According to Doug, the aircraft's accelerometer recorded 14 g! I cannot vouch for the veracity of this story but Doug swore it was true. He certainly had a small scar over one eye, where the surgeons had presumably opened him up to see if all the relevant parts were still connected. It seemed to affect neither his high spirits nor his eyesight – nor his taste for gin. Apparently the Hunter was fine, which proves what strong machines Sidney Camm designed.

Eric Bennett showed me around the cockpit and off I went on a familiarization flight and I was very impressed. Tammy Syme, another Venom pilot from the 'Colonies' (he had been in Aden), and I were allowed about six hours of familiarization flying before the start of the course proper. On one of the early flights, a high-level navigation exercise, I was supposed to rendezvous with Alec Rennie in another Hunter over Birmingham or somewhere in the Midlands, but I could not see him so I flew on alone to West Raynham. About five minutes after I landed, Rennie's engine flamed out when he was on the final approach and he ejected. However, something had gone wrong with the explosive bolts which were supposed to blow off the cockpit canopy and the poor fellow was killed. I understand the investigators found a manufacturing fault. The reason for the flame-out was also discovered. On the right-hand side of the cockpit were two switches and two 'doll's eye' indicators. The switches were to feed fuel from the wing tanks to the engine, and they were both found to be selected to off. The engine had stopped simply because it was starved of fuel. That demonstrated the importance of pre-flight cockpit checks.

The course lasted for two months and included fighter-versus-fighter combat, attacks against jet bombers and ground-attack missions. A staff pilot or two would always be in the formation and comprehensive debriefings were held after each sortie. When the course was over, I was told I had come out top. Tammy went off to Duxford as a flight commander on No. 65 Squadron and I slowly wended my way south through East Anglia on a very foggy night in my Alfa 1900.

The mess anteroom fire at North Weald was a welcome sight. It was now early December 1957 and I was back on Treble One for my fifth fighter tour. It felt good to be back at North Weald, but times had changed. Nos. 601 and 604 squadrons had been disbanded, of course, and the whole place had a run-down air. It seemed that whatever cash was available was going to the V Force of Bomber Command.

Our Hunter Mk 6s were good aircraft and the four 30 mm Aden cannons were devastating close-range weapons, but what we really needed in addition to the cannons were a couple of Sidewinder air-to-air missiles because the Hunter's performance was becoming marginal against a modern jet bomber. Why, oh why, was the 'thin wing' Hunter not produced? This was our quickest and cheapest route to a genuinely supersonic fighter. As I understand it, this machine could have been in service not much later than the Mk 6 and would have been at least as good as the American F100 Super Sabre and probably better. I gather that Hawkers had done a great deal of work on this project and nearly went ahead with it as a private venture. I feel that if they had, it could have been an export success like its 'older brother'. More than twenty air forces had bought the Hunter. And what happened to the other Hawker project, the 1121, which they were going to call the Hurricane? From photographs of the mock-up it looked like a big F-16 and was projected to be a Mach 2 plus aircraft with multi-role capability and a 2,500 mile ferry range without in-flight refuelling – and all this was going on in the 1950s!

Thanks to Mr Duncan Sandys and, later, Mr Harold Wilson's government, we got nothing and were obliged to make a supersonic fighter out of a high-speed research aircraft. The English Electric P1 became the Lightning – a lovely aircraft to fly, with an excellent performance, but it was not designed in the first place as a combat aircraft. It was short on range and endurance and was not very reliable in its early days. A ground engineer once likened its hydraulic system to a bowl of spaghetti. When it was wisely decided that it needed cannons to back up the air-to-air missiles, they had to be fitted in an external gun-pack. The auxiliary jettisonable fuel tanks had to be fitted on top of the wings. I suppose they worked all right, but they looked ridiculous. In the meantime the powerful economy of the USA allowed them to go ahead with their Century series fighters and the French took a good look at our Fairy Delta research aircraft and went ahead to produce their excellent Dassault Mirage.

Later, Hawker's supersonic version of the Harrier, the 1154, was cancelled, as were the tactical transport aircraft and the TSR2. An unfortunate side effect of all this was the continuous drain of our skilled engineers and scientists to more progressive and lucrative jobs overseas. I suppose all our money was going to the Concorde, the National Health Service and the V Force. We pilots in Fighter Command were now the poor relations. The Bomber boys even had cafeterias at their dispersals. We referred to them as 'Eating Command' or 'The Great White Detergent' – sour grapes, I suppose. I personally felt that those big, white, four engined machines were too vulnerable, as well as being very expensive. Had the enormous losses of Bomber Command in the Second World War been forgotten? What we now had were a few modern Lancaster types when what we really needed were a lot of modern Mosquito types. That was my theory at the time, and I believe the fact that the big monsters disappeared and the RAF was eventually equipped with the multi-role, two seat Tornado supports my theory. However, it is interesting to speculate that we might have had the Mach 2.2 Hawker 1121 by the late sixties and, who knows, it might have been a winner. Sir Sydney Camm usually got it right. As things worked out it almost seems that the British aircraft industry was for a while controlled by the Kremlin.

Roger Topp was still in charge of the squadron but only Colin Hardie was left from 1954. The others had all moved on and Dave Garrett had been killed in a mid-air collision the previous year. The remaining winter months were taken up with a mixture of tactical training and formation aerobatic practice. Paddy Hine from my Tangmere days was there, as was Frank Travers-Smith, formerly of No. 60 Squadron, Tengah.

My return to North Weald was shortlived; on 20 February 1958, the squadron moved to North Luffenham, where we had the whole airfield and a huge, modern officers' mess to ourselves. The Canadian fighter wing had left years before and North Luffenham had then become the night fighter OTU. That had now closed down, a sign of the times.

The Black Arrows aerobatic team of No. 111 Squadron had received a great deal of acclaim over the previous year. Roger Topp had introduced some common-sense principles to display flying. One was to display the plan view of the formation for the maximum possible time, because only in plan view did a formation look right. Another was to position the formation so that the spectators did not have to crane their necks more than 45 degrees in any direction to keep it in sight. Considerable allowance had to be made for the wind conditions. Was the wind blowing towards or away from the crowd? When should the smoke be used to best effect? A lot of teams overdo the use of smoke and end up hiding themselves from view behind it. For example, it is not much use blowing out smoke on the way up in a loop because that means you are going to be invisible on the way down.

Formation aerobatics are inherently dangerous, there is no denying the fact, and the number of accidents suffered throughout the world by so many national aerobatic teams is sobering. The concentration required is absolutely total and the mutual trust between the team members has to be 100 per cent. As the numbers increase, so does the difficulty, in an ever-steepening curve. Is it all worth it? Well, there is no denying that it is a great way to 'show the flag' and give taxpayers some idea of what they are getting for their money – there is no way they can see skilful interceptions taking place at 48,000 ft, 200 miles out over the North Sea. At some of the huge air displays in Europe in the fifties and sixties, it was a real battle for prestige, with up to seven or eight national teams competing. The competition was not official, but it was always there. The unsung heroes, as usual were the ground crew. The serviceability requirements of the big teams of No. 111 and 92 Squadrons were such that Herculean efforts were required by the ground engineers. They never let us down.

The aerobatic pilots on Treble One, apart from the CO and myself, were Paddy Hine, Matt Kemp, Ron Smith, Les Swart, Bob Barcilon, Dick Clayton-Jones, Norman Lamb, 'Oscar' Wild, Roger Hymans, 'Chas' Boyer, 'Oakie' Oakford, 'Chan' Biss, Tony Aldridge, Dave Edmondson, Mike Thurley, and later Chris Strong, Alan Brindle and from No. 60 Squadron, Frank Grimshaw. As spring arrived, we increased the amount of formation aerobatic practice. I usually flew as number seven, number six or number two. I also did some leading of a team of five aircraft. The basic formations at this stage were of nine or five aircraft. On 30 April 1958, I flew four sorties of air-to-air photography in a Meteor 14. Sitting behind me was Mr Mike Chase or Mr Dovey from the Air Ministry. It must have been very difficult to handle the big camera at 3–4 g during looping manoeuvres. I did four more of these sorties on 7 and 8 May. The Meteor 14 was a nice aeroplane; it had a bubble canopy giving better visibility than the Meteor 11. Its AI radar had about twice the range of the old Mk 10, but it still would not do more than Mach 0.82 and there were still no ejection seats.

The team of nine went off to Stavanger, Norway, but my first display was at the USAF base at Spangdalam in Germany. We did further displays at Bentwaters, Alconbury and Bitburg before moving to our new permanent home at Wattisham in Suffolk on 18 June 1958. Wattisham was to remain the home of the squadron for many years.

On 20 June we flew to St. Nazaire in Brittany for a display at Rennes on 21 June. This was interesting because the show was in honour of former members of the French Resistance and a very nice, friendly bunch they were. We were all impressed with Mlle Colette Duval, a stunt parachutist. The poor lady was limping badly as she had been blown into a graveyard by a wind gust and had hurt her ankle.

On 26 June we were off again, this time to Biercet, near Liège in Belgium. This was a very big show, attended by King Bauduoin. A few things stuck in my mind from this display. It was the first time I saw the F-104 Starfighter. There were two of them, both having flown the Atlantic using in-flight refuelling. Their wings looked like two razor blades they were so small and it was then that I realized just how far behind we had fallen. The F-104 turned out to be less than perfect but the fact remains that it was twice as fast as a Hunter!

The weather conditions were difficult. The cloud base was satisfactory, about 4,000 ft but the visibility was very poor in industrial haze and I estimated it as less than 2 miles. We were able to do our normal show, although it would not have been very easy for Roger Topp in the lead. I was number seven that day. The American team, the Skyblazers, had a more difficult time in their F100 Super Sabres, which were far less manoeuverable than our Hunters, so their display looked a bit tame. Their leader, Captain Bill Creech, a nice chap that we got to know well, was ticked off more or less in public, by General Curtis Le May, 'Old Iron Pants', which seemed pretty unfair to us. We were all presented with a brass medallion by King Baudouin but what really stuck in my mind was an incident at the end of our display. I was walking back from our dispersal with Paddy Hine, and Ron Smith was a few paces ahead of us. The Italian team, the *Diavoli Rossi* was just completing their show. Suddenly, directly in front of us, head-on, came an Italian F-84, fast and very low. He could not have been higher than 6 ft above the ground. Paddy and I 'hit the deck' but Ron Smith, in an amazing display of *sang-froid*, continued to walk forward, with one hand raised in a 'Churchillian salute'; the Italian was obliged to ease up a little.

The Italians could always be relied upon to give a spirited display; low and fast was their motto. I remember once seeing their rear man in a line-astern loop having to move into line-abreast on the aircraft ahead of him to avoid hitting some trees. Their leader in those days was a piratical-looking figure with a small moustache and a scar on one cheek. He reminded me of Bob Stanford-Tuck, the famous RAF fighter pilot from the Second World War. The Italian fighting man got a lot of bad press from our propagandists during the war, but the courage of their naval frogmen and fighter pilots was never in doubt. Ray Hesslyn, the renowned New Zealand

Spitfire pilot, once told me that when he was flying from Malta, his most dangerous adversary was an Italian flying a Macchi 202.

On our return to England on 30 June, we were obliged to land at Tangmere to be inspected by the customs officer to ensure that no one had exceeded the cigarette and alcohol allowance – hardly a cost-effective exercise I would have thought.

During July 1958 I did a lot of leading formation aerobatic practices and flew as number two on several shows. The big show that month was at Soesterberg in Holland. Several other national teams were present and it was a nice sunny day. There was a huge party in the Dutch officers' mess after the show. Prince Bernhardt was present, together with the Dutch Swing College Band and a group of lively Canadian pilots. The evening passed in a haze of songs, laughter and general mayhem.

The quality of the Soesterberg party can be judged by the following incident. I was having a quiet breakfast with Ron Smith when one of our pilots approached the table and said, 'Hello chaps, I've just heard a funny story. It seems one of our fellows was woken in the night when some lost soul entered his room, wandered about a bit and then peed in the wardrobe.' Ron fixed the newcomer with a frosty stare and replied, 'I don't know what you're laughing about. It was my room and you're the one who did it.'

Later, we flew home in a most subdued manner. Over the North Sea, some RAF fighters intercepted our formation. If they were looking forward to a dogfight then they were disappointed, as we sensibly restricted ourselves to a gentle rocking of wings to indicate that they had not caught us by surprise.

In August 1958, Roger Topp got permission to try out the huge 22-aircraft formation for the Farnborough display. We borrowed some extra Hunters and volunteer pilots from other squadrons to make up the numbers. The extra pilots only had to fly in a line-astern position, traditionally the least demanding spot, and it all worked out better than expected. The first manoeuvre was a double loop with twenty-two aircraft. The second loop could be a little tighter than the first as positive g was already on as the loop started. Three of the volunteers from each rear flank broke away towards the end of the second loop. That left sixteen aircraft to complete a formation barrel roll. After a further loop, seven aircraft broke away, leaving nine. After a further loop, four bomb-bursted away, leaving the basic five team to complete the show. Afterwards, all twenty-two aircraft plus two airborne spares, recovered to Odiham, where we were based for the Farnborough week. The aviation world was amazed. The 22-aircraft formation shape was not very pretty, but it was certainly impressive.

The Royal Navy were there with their Sea Hawk team. They had a spectacular beginning on the first day, when Lieutenant Roger Dimmock had to eject. He was safe but there was an ugly pillar of black smoke off the edge of the airfield. The week went well after that, except on the Wednesday when low cloud and rain restricted our display to only five aircraft.

Two days after returning from Farnborough we were off to Bordeaux. I cannot remember much about that show, which must have been straightforward, but I do recall the spectacular mosquitoes. I got a bite on my face which developed into a boil-sized pustule. One of the pilots, I think 'Oakie' Oakford, suffered a bite which completely closed one eye.

Following the Battle of Britain displays at Biggin Hill, Wattisham Honnington and Odiham, the aerobatic season came to a close and we became busy with Exercise Sunbeam, that year's air defence exercise. Roger Topp left the squadron, having been the CO for the best part of four years, and in October 1958, Pete Latham arrived to take command.

The winter of 1958/9 was devoted to the usual mix of tactical training and formation aerobatic practice. We had a pleasant detachment up to Leuchars for some concentrated air-to-air firing and some of the pilots had a memorably riotous weekend at the Loch Earne Head Hotel. On a flight from Leuchars back to Wattisham, I had a strange 'sixth sense' experience. While flying at 40,000 ft I suddenly felt that something was not right. The instrument readings were all normal and there did not seem to be any other aircraft about, but I still had a feeling of unease. Something made me look straight up and there, right over my aircraft, no more than 100 ft above me, was a Vulcan V Bomber. I got out of there in a hurry.

Pete Latham took over the reins with little fuss. An early tendency to vary his rate of roll whilst leading the formation gave us a couple of frights, but that was soon overcome and he became a very competent leader. His relaxed and jovial personality also helped. One thing had improved on Treble One. Nearly all the pilots on the squadron were now involved in the aerobatic team. In the earlier days this was not so and the pilots who were not in the team definitely had the feeling that they were second class citizens, which naturally affected their morale.

We shared the airfield at Wattisham with No. 41 Squadron, a night-fighter unit flying Javelins – a machine which never appealed to me. There is a story that an American officer inspecting an early version at Farnborough looked in amazement at the thickness of the wing and said, 'Boy, that's the best advert for thrust I've ever seen.' I always had the feeling that the navy got the better night fighter in the Sea Vixen. No. 41 Squadron had a bad day at Wattisham. One of their pilots on his last flight,an American on exchange and due to return to the USA, decided to do a loop over the airfield and did not make it. The navigator ejected but he was killed.

For us the good life continued at Wattisham. The station commander was extremely popular. He was a South African, Teddy Morris. At one dining-in night, the AOC, Air Vice Marshal Foord-Kelsey remarked that Teddy Morris seemed like a relaxed version of Perry Como. I was doing more formation leading now and we were investigating some routines of co-ordinated aerobatics. Pete Latham would lead nine and I would lead five. My lot was Blue Section, referred to by Roger Hymans as the 'Blue Burgers' – usually myself, Roger Hymans, Norman Lamb, 'Oakie' Oakford and Tony Aldridge. However it was not until later in the year that we really got to work on the sixteen formation and the normal displays were still done with nine aircraft. We did a lot of displays in England but the most memorable ones were in Europe.

On 10 April, 1959 we went to the US fighter base at Bitburg in Germany. As I climbed out of my aircraft, a car drew up and out came a jolly, bouncy man in a colonel's uniform.

'Hi there,' he said. 'I'm Colonel Walter B. Putnam, you can call me Benny.' It was a most friendly greeting from the base commander. We were invited to the crew room of one of the F-100 squadrons for coffee, and they showed us a movie they had made. It was a silent film called *The New Head*, and was just about the funniest home movie I have ever seen. The opening scene showed a row of pilots in flying gear standing with their backs to the camera. In the distance rose a familiar column of black smoke. The caption at the bottom of the screen said, 'Goddamn it, best ping pong player we ever had.' The film lasted for about twenty minutes and the black humour had us all in fits of laughter.

Our display next day went as normal and all the 'usual suspects' were there, including the Skyblazers and the French and Italian teams. That night the Americans gave us all a formal dinner in their officers' club, which was rather different from the British equivalent. People actually lit up cigars between the soup and fish. Following the usual toasts to the heads of state of the attending officers, Colonel Putnam made a speech during which he awarded the same accolade to all the teams, Most Improved Team This Year. He then continued, 'Now we come to the RAF. When you guys disappeared behind the trees, the general turned to me and said, "Well Benny, it looks like you just bought the farm".'

Things got lively after dinner. A very large silver tureen was filled with champagne, we all dipped our glasses into it and toast after toast was proposed to all the countries represented. This went on for some time as the champagne level slowly lowered. Finally, all the toasts exhausted, one of our pilots picked up the tureen and two-handedly took a swig. It was then passed around the RAF pilots, ending finally in Pete Latham's hands. He drained the last drops, placed the tureen on his head and then slowly sank to the floor with his back to the wall, wearing a happy smile. That more or less concluded our visit to Bitburg. I recall that Pete required some assistance to find his quarters.

On 24 May, 1959 we were scheduled to give a nine-aircraft display at Rygge, the military airfield close to Oslo. I was flying as number six or seven. A couple of weeks before that I had managed to break two of the metacarpal bones in my right hand. A day or two later, with my forearm, wrist and part of my hand in plaster, I had a discussion with Pete Latham to debate my fitness for formation aerobatics. I thought I would be all right, with just a change of technique, as I could not flex my wrist.

My assessment proved to be correct so off we went on 22 May to Jever on the North German coast to refuel and stay overnight. We also wanted to pick up a crate of Scotch whisky to take to the Norwegian air force mess. The Norwegian pilots would appreciate that as whisky in Norway was so expensive, it was like liquid gold. That evening as we were all enjoying a couple of pints in the mess bar at Jever, Clayton-Jones, always called CJ and a very brave officer, decided he would show us his famous trick, perfected during his previous tour at Jever. The idea was to build a column of six bar stools and climb up them to a balcony over the bar. He got as far as the fifth when the whole edifice collapsed depositing C.J. on the carpet. We picked him up, dusted him down and asked if he was all right. He said he was, but he did not think he could walk. So it proved and he was carried off to bed by Roger Hymans and another pilot. The next morning he announced that he still could not walk but he could definitely fly. He was literally carried to his Hunter and deposited in the cockpit. Off we went to Oslo and on arrival performed a few loops and rolls, trailing white smoke against the blue sky, announcing our arrival in spectacular fashion. As we taxied to the hard standing, shut down the engines and opened the canopies, I noticed two American air force colonels standing on the edge of the tarmac. One of them had a cold cigar butt between his lips. When he saw me climb out of my cockpit with the white plaster cast in view, he removed the cigar butt from his mouth and turned towards his companion with a startled expression. Then CJ whistled for assistance and two ground crew lifted him out of his cockpit and carried him away. The colonel turned once more to his colleague and spoke only one long drawn-out word: 'Goddamn.'

Quite so, I thought. What more could one say? By that evening CJ was fully mobile and the display went off well on the following day.

Another show in May was at Wiesbaden. Some 'new boys' were performing there, as well as the regular cast. The Greek air force had shown up with their F-86s. I looked into one of their cockpits and was rather surprised to see several holes in the instrument panel, which should have held instruments! After our display we were enjoying a cold beer in a hospitality tent when one of our pilots walked in and said, 'Hey chaps, the Greeks are trying to land seven in formation.' 'Bloody hell,' was the comment from one of our team as we all went towards the exit.

'Where are you guys going?' asked an American.

'To watch the prang,' was the reply.

Wiesbaden had a rather narrow runway and the surface was pretty rough. Sure enough the inevitable happened. The Greeks touched down and shortly thereafter one F-86 hit another. They both left the runway and one hit a small concrete structure. Luckily no one was badly hurt but the Greek air force inventory was down by at least one F-86.

Our next overseas visit was to Lisbon. On 9 June we set off for Bordeaux, our refuelling stop. We let down over the Bay of Biscay and flew at low level up the Garonne River. We had a brief period of consternation as we could get no reply on the radio from the French air traffic control. Eventually we did, and the refuelling stop passed without further incident. It was British Trade Week in Lisbon, attended by Princess Margaret. We lived in the Portuguese officers' mess in town and had two very pleasant days there. Our display took place over the Tagus River right in front of the city, and during the show we did a roll in one direction followed by another in the opposite direction. By a sheer fluke our smoke trails left a perfect letter 'M'. Everyone thought it was for 'Margaret' and it was declared to be very clever by the VIPs. Naturally we did not disillusion them.

There was a reception that night for the princess aboard a British liner, the *Andes*. We never even saw her, she was so hemmed-in by a crush of people. I enjoyed several glasses of wine outside a bistro and rode back in a taxi with Roger

Hymans. We both got a fit of the giggles as we sang some of Tom Lehrer's songs – the wine must have been very strong. The return journey via Bordeaux was straightforward; some Spanish fighters tried a practice interception over Galicia, but they could not catch us. A few nights later we were all enjoying some Portuguese brandy in the bar we decided it was just as good as Remy Martin. We were wrong; the next morning we all suffered from monumental headaches.

Our next stop was the big Paris Air Show at Le Bourget, where we performed with nine aircraft on 20 and 21 June. There were a few notable incidents during this visit. There was a fatal crash when an Italian Fiat G91 slammed into the ground in the undershoot area. The French, in true Gallic fashion, told us to move our aircraft to another part of the airfield but we were not allowed to start our engines. It was obviously not practical to push nine aircraft $^1/_2$ mile or so. How were we to solve this dilemma? Among the aircraft at Le Bourget was a very large Ilyushin or Tupolev turbo-prop machine – a very handsome aircraft, although we thought the wrinkles on the wing skin looked a bit ominous. Accompanying it was a little Russian chap in a flat cap with a tractor. After a brief negotiation, he towed all our aircraft for us. Could this have been the first tiny crack in the Iron Curtain?

We did a nine-aircraft formation take-off on the second day because the French or the Italians had done one with seven so we had to top that. I kept my reservations about unrehearsed manoeuvres to myself and it went well. After the final bomb-burst manoeuvre we re-formed into close formation as we circled the Eiffel Tower at about 600 ft. There were the usual cocktail parties to attend, and there was Basil, my old

The author at RAF Leconfield in 1962.

No 4 FTS Tiger Moths in formation over Southern Rhodesia in 1948.

The author in a Harvard at Heany in Southern Rhodesia in 1949.

A Mk 6 Mosquito at Brize Norton in 1950.

A Mk 36 Mosquito night fighter RL 179. The author flew this aircraft eleven times operating out of Tangmere during Exercise Emperor in October 1950.

Meteor NF 11s of No 29 Squadron off the Sussex coast in 1952.

Meteor Mk 8s of No 56 Squadron in 1953.

This is taken from camera gun film of a banner target at a dangerously low angle-off. The author was flying the Meteor tug in the photograph and was singularly unimpressed when he saw the film. No 56 Squadron 1953.

Pilots of No 60 Squadron at Tengah in Singapore in 1956.
Left to right: The author, F/O Mick Mercer, F/O John Pusey, Flt Lt Bob Price, Flt Lt Pete Cornish, F/O Bob Johnson, F/O Geof Bradshaw, F/O Terry Kingswood, Flt Lt David Black and F/O David Ryles.

60 Squadron aerobatic team flying over Malaya during 1956.

A Venom FB4 starting up for a bandit strike in 1957. Note the 1,000 lb bomb under the wing.

Blue Section of No 111 Squadron in 1958.

This painting was based on a photograph taken of 22 Hunters of No 111 Squadron over Farnborough in September 1958.

The Black Arrows aerobatic team of No 111 Squadron in 1959. *Rear - left to right:* Stan Wood, Frank Travers-Smith, Dave Edmondson, 'Chas' Boyer. *Middle:* Dick Clayton-Jones, Paddy Hine, Pete Latham, Matt Kemp, 'Oscar' Wild. *Front:* 'Oakie' Oakfield, Roger Hymans, Brian Mercer, Norman Lamb and Tony Aldridge.

A Hunter Mk 6 and the 1933 Alf Romeo at Middleton St George in 1961.

Tight Five. Blue Diamond Hunters over Cyprus in 1961.

Blue Diamonds over Middleton St George in 1961.

This formation was first displayed by the Blue Diamonds at Furstenfeldbrack, Munich, in October 1961.

Erich Hartmann. The world's number one fighter ace, taken around 1944.

The author with Crown Prince Constantine of Greece in 1961.

This photograph was taken during the Blue Diamond's display at Farnborough in 1961. The photographer in the right-hand seat of the author's T7 Hunter was Wing Commander Tony Bartley DFC*, a distinguished pilot of 92 Squadron during the Battle of Britain. The formation of 16 aircraft is entering a right-hand turn following a loop.

16 Hunters of No 92 Squadron formed the fly-past at the inauguration of the Trenchard Memorial by the Prime Minister, The Rt. Hon. Harold McMillan, in Whitehall on the 19th of July 1961.

Diamond 16 of 92 Squadron as published in the Illustrated London News in 1961.

The Blue Diamonds at Biggin Hill, Battle of Britain Day, 1961.

The RAF Gunnery Team in 1962. *Back - Left to right:* Peter Highton, the author (also team leader) and Piet van Wyk. *Front:* Tony Aldridge and Johnny Walker.

This photograph was taken on 19 June 2005 at Kemble Air Day. *From left to right:* Piet van Wyk, the author and Tony Aldridge. The aircraft is the recently restored and flying Hunter T7 XL577 (G-BXKF) painted in Blue Diamond colours.

John Griffiths, 92 Squadron Engineering Officer, seen talking with senior NCOs at Leeuwarden in 1962.

The author receiving the Guynemer Trophy from Prince Bernhardt at Leeuwarden in 1962. Air Chief Marshal The Earl of Bandon is in the Khaki uniform.

A happy return to Leconfield after winning the Guynemer Trophy. The author is being greeted by the AOC, Air Vice Marshal Clayton.

Back from Leeuwarden and in the officer's mess at Leconfield with the Guyener Trophy. *Left to right:* Tony Aldridge, Pete Highton, Piet van Wyk, the author, John Griffiths and Mike Davis.

The 14 Hunters of the Blue Diamonds in 1962.

The Blue Diamonds over the Yorkshire coast.

The Blue Diamonds descending in a loop over Yorkshire.

A Cathay Pacific Convair 880 - the author's 'four-engine fighter'.

Boeing 747 freighters of Air Hong Kong at Kai Tak in 1993.

A Cathay Pacific Boeing 747 on the approach to runway 13 at Kai Tak in Hong Kong.

Flying a Harvard again - the author in the cockpit of an ex-US Navy aircraft at Bryan Field, Texas in 1986.

A picture and heading from a magazine published in 2001. Forty years later the shadow of the Black Arrows was still in evidence. Even a casual glance will reveal this formation to be the Blue Diamonds.

navigator, looking splendid and doing his diplomatic stuff in his capacity as Assistant Air Attaché. Clayton-Jones and Dave Edmondson decided to climb the Eiffel Tower the hard way, by ladder, but had to quit about two-thirds of the way up.

During this visit I met one of my father's old teaching colleagues whom I had last seen when I was still a child before the war. She had married a Frenchman and during the war was involved in the underground escape organization for Allied airmen who had been shot down. The poor lady had been caught and sent to Ravensbruck Concentration Camp. She was a very nice person and certainly very lucky to survive that experience.

Back at base we continued the usual mixture of tactical flying and formation aerobatic work. In July we gave shows at Waterbeach, Bagington, Bawdsey, Marham, Manston, Calais and Tours. The visit to Tours on the River Loire was very pleasant. On the final evening there was a big party in the famous wine storage caves. The French air force decided to have a wine-drinking competition, which was won by a demure-looking lady captain who knocked back an enormous flagon of white wine in one go. She then delicately dabbed her lips with a lace handkerchief and strolled away, looking sober and stable – a very impressive performance which we wisely did not try to emulate.

We were now working on a routine for the 1959 Farnborough Display. Our plan was to use sixteen aircraft initially and then split into a team of nine and one of seven. During August we gave shows at Sylt in north-west Germany and at the French seaside resort of Royan, operating out of Cognac. The island of Sylt was the base of the armament practice camp for the steadily shrinking 2nd Tactical Air

Force. The locals had a small display team of four Meteors. These machines were normally used to tow targets for air-to-air firing practice and shortly before our arrival, they had suffered a fatal mid-air collision.

Pete Latham had been experimenting with a throat microphone. We tried hard to talk him out of it because over the radio he sounded just like Bill and Ben, the Flowerpot Men from the well-known children's TV programme. This was all very well for TV but we needed rather more clarity in his executive orders. About this time he had a crash on his motor scooter. His face came into nasty contact with the gravel and he was *hors de combat* for several days. As a result I found myself leading the team of nine, which I did at Cottesmore, Abingdon and Wolverhampton. After landing at Cottesmore, I was met by the station commander, Group Captain Johnny Johnson, the famous fighter ace from the Second World War. He greeted me with the words, 'Hello Brian, well done. I see that ass end Charlie got a bit close to the trees but then they usually do don't they? Anyway, come and meet the Shah.' He then introduced me to the Shah of Iran, who was visiting the V bomber base at Cottesmore and we had a friendly chat for a few minutes.

The routine for Farnborough was proceeding quite well. One manoeuvre which apparently looked very impressive from the ground was when I broke away from the main formation with my group and then barrel rolled around the remainder, led by Pete Latham. However it was not easy to make it look tidy, and it only worked well about three times out of four, so we had to cancel it. We started off using sixteen aircraft and after a few manoeuvres my seven machines broke away in a bomb-burst, joining up again as the front nine completed more items. At the end, the nine carried out a loop, followed by a downward bomb-burst and my seven then climbed vertically through the smoke trail left by them. We in turn bomb-burst upwards, but the timing was rather tricky. One day we got a bit too close and I found myself leading my seven vertically upwards towards Pete's nine, which for a second or so was still together, heading straight down. Their bomb-burst was followed immediately by ours as we climbed through the air space they had just vacated. It must have looked good, but my pulse rate went up for a while.

After the Battle of Britain displays at Gaydon, Cottesmore, Felixstowe and Wattisham, the display flying was over for 1959, and we reverted to full-time operational practice. However, the year had one more dramatic moment in store for me.

On 13 December, I climbed into my Hunter to go air firing. We were up at Aklington for our annual armament camp. After the normal cockpit and safety checks, I lifted up the master electrical gang-switch and two 30 mm cannons opened fire. Before I could bang the switch down, about twenty shells had whistled across the airfield and right through the dispersal of No. 66 Squadron. By a miracle they missed everything and simply buried themselves somewhere in the Northumberland earth. Pete Bairsto, the CO of No. 66 Squadron, showing commendable aplomb under the circumstances, rang up the No. 111 dispersal and said, 'If you'll give us a few minutes we'll arm up and fire back!'

Of course a board of enquiry was set up straight away. In order for the cannons to be fired on the ground, a switch down on the floor of the cockpit called the butt test switch had to be operated, as normally the firing circuit is inhibited when the aircraft weight is on the wheels. The board members did not seem to believe me when I assured them that I had not operated this switch, nor had I moved the gun trigger from its safe position or tested the camera gun button. Unfortunately the ground engineers could not find a fault in the firing circuit and I started to get a bit worried. Eventually it was decided to fly the aircraft down to Chivenor, where they had some proper test firing butts. I took the aircraft down there and we set everything up as before. The Chivenor armament officer and his crew put on tin hats and took up safe positions. I put up the master switch again and once more the cannons opened fire. This time they only fired off about ten rounds before I knocked off the switch. A much more thorough investigation was carried out and the fault was found. There was a short which had something to do with the circuit operating the pump that squirted out the diesel fuel we used to make smoke. This fuel was in a tank mounted in the aircraft ammunition bay and the pump was operated by the gun trigger.

The year was coming to an end and my second tour on Treble One was just about over. There was talk of an exchange posting to the US Air Force. There was a place coming up at George Air Force Base in California flying F-100s, but it never happened. On the 1st of January 1960 I was promoted out of the chance of an exchange posting to the USAF as I was now a squadron leader. I was also awarded the Air Force Cross so that was mostly good news. Then I was told that I was to work for the Director of Recruiting as a schools liaison officer in Yorkshire and that literally brought me down to earth.

CHAPTER EIGHT

Schools Liaison

In January 1960 I found myself in a gloomy, Dickensian office in the Leeds RAF recruiting centre. In walked Squadron Leader Paddy King, fresh from an exchange tour with the USAF Tactical Air Command. He had been flying F-101s based on the eastern seaboard of the USA and both of us were rather underwhelmed with our situation. However it turned out to be not so bad after all.

We lived at Church Fenton with a group H.Q. of Flying Training Command; the fighter wing had long gone. Our team of school liaison officers was completed by Flying Officer Valerie Webster, WRAF. Valerie liked to refer to Paddy and myself as 'my squadron leaders.' The three of us shared an RAF Standard Vanguard, a film projector, lots of films and several boxes of pamphlets. We had to cover all the schools in Yorkshire; I concentrated mostly on the West Riding area. It was a novel experience which made me feel a bit like a travelling salesman. Some of the headmasters were quite enthusiastic, some were pacifists and reluctant to let us through their doors; however we always knew where we stood with Yorkshire folk. They were always straightforward with us. I got quite a lot of public-speaking practice, addressing school assemblies, Rotary Clubs, Duke of

Edinburgh Award presentations, etc. My most daunting task was addressing the whole body of a girls' high school in Scarborough. The formidable headmistress shared the rostrum with me and the sea of young female faces gazing up from the floor of the hall was quite intimidating. I got this duty because Valerie was sick – I was very relieved when she came back on duty!

The good news at Church Fenton was that Joe Blyth was also there on the group staff and there was an aeroplane to fly, a piston engined Provost. It was a delightful machine, fully aerobatic, and I was able to fly it regularly. The other good thing was that during school holidays I went back to fly with Treble One, thanks to Peter Latham.

I spent all of August 1960 flying out of Wattisham and on four of the Farnborough displays in September, I had the novel experience of flying as number sixteen in the aerobatic team. So the Black Arrows that year had a squadron leader at the front and another one right at the back. I found the relative lack of responsibility quite relaxing, but it was noisy. The fifteen Rolls Royce Avons in front of me made a surprising din even in my pressurized cockpit.

I owned a rather nice 1933 supercharged Alfa Romeo Gran Sport that I had bought from Bunty Scott Moncrieff for £500. I clumsily over-revved it one day right outside the brewery in Tadcaster, and stripped the timing gears. However I knew that the owner of one of the big car distributors in Leeds owned a blown 2.3 Alfa of similar vintage to mine, so I rang him up and asked if his mechanics could fix it for me. Some weeks later I went to collect it. 'How much do I owe you?' I asked.

'Nothing,' said the garage owner. 'We have had your car parked in our showroom and it brought so many people in to see it that we got a lot of extra business.' I have generally been lucky with my more exotic cars over the years. I have owned two Maseratis, a Ferrari, a brace of Aston Martins and a couple of Bentleys – all second hand of course. I had no disasters and nearly all of them were sold at a profit. The classic Alfa was sold for £550 in 1962.

One car stands out in my memory as being years ahead of its time. It was a late series Lancia Aurelia GT that I bought from Duncan Hamilton, and it would not feel old-fashioned today.

After the summer, I was all set to renew my recruiting drive in the Yorkshire schools again. I felt some sense of irony that I was pushing the glories of the RAF, at a time when our politicians seemed determined to wreck it. Before I could take up my duties again, however, I had a most intriguing phone call. I was to report forthwith to the Commander-in-Chief (C-in-C) of Fighter Command, Air Marshal Sir Hector McGregor, at Bentley Priory. I was on the threshold of the best two years of my entire flying career.

CHAPTER NINE

No. 92 Squadron and the Blue Diamonds

Treble One was about to re-equip with Lightnings and it was therefore decided to hand over the role of the aerobatic squadron to another unit. Someone had to lead the new team for 1961 and it was decided that it would be me. I believe it was thanks to Group Captain Teddy Morris that I got the job and I shall always be grateful to him.

So, I found myself in the C-in-C's office with the Senior Air Staff Officer, the Senior Technical Staff Officer and the Senior Administrative Staff Officer.

'Right, Mercer,' said the C-in-C. 'You are to take command of 92 Squadron at Middleton St George. We are shortly sending the squadron out to Cyprus for a couple of months; we expect you to come back from that detachment with an aerobatic team. Now, what do you need?'

This seemed too good to be true, so I said, 'Could I have a few of the 111 Squadron pilots to form the nucleus of the team?' The answer was yes to that and I was to get Chris Strong, Tony Aldridge, Chan Biss and Frank Grimshaw. 'If there are any new, inexperienced pilots on the squadron, could they be posted to other squadrons?' I said. I did not want any 'second-class citizens' on No. 92, I wanted every pilot to be involved, because that was the key to high morale.

'We can do that,' said the C-in-C. 'Anything else?'

I then explained that because of the very high serviceability requirement, we needed a first-rate squadron engineering officer and I thought it would be a good idea to have a couple of NCOs from Treble One who were already imbued with the high serviceability spirit. 'What about that?' said the C-in-C to the Senior Technical Staff Officer. 'Who is the best engineering officer we have?'

'Probably John Griffiths up at Duxford,' was the reply.

As a result I got John Griffiths and Flight Sergeant O'Brien, who were both superb, and also a very good corporal from Treble One. The C-in-C then said he would like to know my ideas for the aircraft colour scheme soon. The meeting ended with these words: 'Right, Mercer, we have given you what you have asked for so go and do the job and don't have any accidents.' This was accompanied by a penetrating stare, and I was left in no doubt that my future would be bleak if we had a crash. A few months earlier, Flight Lieutenant Stan Wood of the Black Arrows had been killed in a mid-air collision.

I left for Middleton St. George to take over No. 92 from Bob Dixon – The '92nd Foot and Mouth' of Battle of Britain fame. Some famous names had served on 92: Bob Stanford-Tuck, Brian Kingcombe, Johnny Kent, Tony Bartley, Roger Bushell, Titch Havercroft and others. The squadron had fought a very good war and had been one of the two Fighter Command squadrons to fly the American F-86 in the 1950s.

Bob Dixon had led a small aerobatic team as a back-up to Treble One during 1960 but we were now to become the 'first eleven,' and we were all looking forward to it. I have a theory about fighter squadrons: they normally contain three categories of pilots. Group A is a small handful of the best ones, good aircraft handlers, good shots and full of self-confidence. They are the ones who account for most of the enemy in a war. Group B form the majority of the pilots. They are the standard, average chaps who do their job competently and reliably. Then we have Group C, the smallest group. These pilots are the ones who can't shoot, get separated from their formations, lack self-confidence and have more than their share of aircraft problems. In a war, these pilots might just as well stay on the ground. In the Second World War, they were Messerschmitt meat.

The great strength of No. 92 Squadron was that we had no 'Category C' pilots, mainly because of the high average experience level. I support Chuck Yeager's theory that there is no substitute for experience; that is what enables pilots to elevate themselves from one category to the next.

During the Battle of Britain, pilots with only ten hours' flying on a Hurricane or Spitfire, who had never fired their guns, were sent into action. This was very wrong. All these poor devils did was provide targets for the German fighter pilots, whose average experience level was higher than ours. Bravery without skill counts for little in a modern war. The ability to shoot well is an essential requirement for a fighter pilot. We were very fortunate indeed that the BF109s did not carry a jettisonable auxiliary fuel tank. If they had, it is not inconceivable that the history of the world over the past sixty years would have been very different. Luckily for our side the German single-seat fighters were very short of endurance.

At Middleton St George we had a farewell party for Bob Dixon, the next time I saw him was in the RAF Club many years later. The former Treble One pilots arrived, Bill Stoker came from one of the Hunter squadrons in Germany, and we all gradually got to know each other. Chan Biss and 'Taff' Freeman were to be rock steady flying as number two and three. There was also Brian St Clair, Dick Calvert (a very nice chap, but only just good enough to be a display pilot), George Aylett, 'Chips' Carpenter, Derek Gill, Jerry Seavers, Hamid Anwar (our exchange officer from the Pakistan Air Force and a very competent aviator), Brian Alchin, Don Oakden (from No. 65 Squadron), Bob Roberts, Crawford Cameron and Pete Taylor (from No. 19 Squadron). We were all different, but it was a very happy band of brothers.

The station commander was Sandy Johnson, later replaced by Freddie Rothwell. I was usually lucky with my Station Commanders and served under some very good men. The Wing Commander Flying was Wing Commander Browne, a rather less sympathetic figure. We shared the airfield with No. 33 Night Fighter Squadron, who flew Javelins. Their CO was a nice chap called Norman Poole. But their days were numbered as the run-down of the air force continued.

From October 1960 to January 1961 we carried on a mixture of tactical training and aerobatic practice, and finalized our colour scheme. The aircraft were to be a deep royal blue with a white lightning flash down the side of the fuselage. Under the cockpit we had the squadron motif, a maple leaf and a cobra's head superimposed on the squadron's colours, a red and yellow chequerboard. The roundels were to be outlined in white and the red, a white and blue motif on the fin was to be sloped backwards like Treble One's scheme. Finally the wing-tips were to be painted white. This last item was possibly our one aesthetic mistake but those white wing-tips saved our bacon one day, as I shall explain later. The first aircraft was painted by Celon at Bovingdon and the C-in-C gave his approval. All the aircraft were painted over the next few months by Marshalls of Cambridge.

We had a rather difficult winter at Middleton St George, as a smelly industrial haze from Middlesbrough frequently blanketed the airfield and cost us flying time. Then on 9 January we all took off for Orange in the south of France, the first leg of our flight to Nicosia, Cyprus. The Mistral was acting up at Orange and it was very windy, but after refuelling off we went on to Malta and Cyprus. At 40,000 ft over the blue Mediterranean the formation looked quite wonderful, as all the aircraft were producing dense white condensation trails. This was definitely better than touring the winter landscape of Yorkshire in a Standard Vanguard. West of Cyprus we were intercepted by some Javelins but we simply turned into their attack to foil them, as we had insufficient fuel for fun and games.

Our welcome at Nicosia was a trifle lukewarm; it seemed that visiting fighter squadrons were not popular. No. 74 Squadron had recently burned the number 74 into the bar carpet, which had not endeared them to the locals. Our arrival in the bar was greeted with the words, 'My God, it's the Cobra squadron; almost as bad as 74,' from the Turkish barman.

The whole place had a rather stuffy air about it and the accommodation left much to be desired. All the airmen and some of the officers had to live in tents, and winter nights in

Cyprus could be quite chilly. However, we pressed on with lots of air-to-air and air-to-ground firing, and rocket firing at the Larnaca range. Our scores were very good. 'Taff' Freemen had volunteered to fly the Meteor 7 target tug out to Cyprus and he arrived a day or two late. He had to fly via El Adem in Libya and got rather short of fuel when the fuel feed from his ventral tank froze up. On my final rocket firing sortie Taff was range safety officer and I managed to get three direct hits in a row. Taff then transmitted the words 'lovely arrows boss'. Unfortunately my fourth rocket missed by fifteen yards and that was the last rocket I ever fired. Those old world War Two three inch rockets were hopelessly obsolete weapons for a modern jet fighter.

During daylight hours we had to keep two fighters armed up and ready for take-off at five minutes' notice. They were called the Battle Flight, although who we were supposed to do battle with was never made clear; the Middle East was having one of its quiet periods.

The Wing Commander Flying, a Coastal Command expert I believe, came into my office in high dudgeon one morning, complaining that my fighters were ruining his tarmac. Rather mystified, I followed him to the damaged area. It was obvious that the culprit had been a Javelin doing a full-power engine test; the jet efflux from a Hunter comes out parallel to the ground so we were obviously not guilty.

We got a lot of good weapons training at Nicosia and our social life was lively. The pilots were going through a darts craze and after flying was over, we all piled into the bar to play our rather weird version. The resident wing commander of the Provost Branch, whom we called Big Mac, enquired what sort of a Mickey Mouse game we were playing. The name of the game then became Mickey Mouse and within a short time it seemed that everyone in the RAF was playing it.

We decided to have a squadron party; Bill Stoker was 'volunteered' to find some girls to liven things up. He succeeded beyond our wildest dreams. On the designated night, there were English girls, French girls, Israeli girls, etc. that Bill had collected from various consulates in Nicosia. The party commenced in the bar, which was separated from the mess anteroom by a wooden partition. It was Friday bingo night in the anteroom and after a while the station adjutant appeared and passed on the station commander's request that we make less noise, as they could not hear the bingo caller. A little later he appeared again to request that we stop firing champagne corks at the partition, so we decided to move the party out of range, to the Ladies Room. It was a truly splendid evening. The displeased station commander kept trying to find me, but we had scouts out and each time he approached I nipped out through the window into the garden, and he never did catch me.

After a month we departed for Akrotiri to get cracking on our aerobatic practice. The move was most welcome, and Akrotiri actually seemed glad to have us. We were made to feel at home by the station commander, Andrew Humphrey. We worked hard there, and four times each day a formation of our Hunters roared off the ground. John Griffiths and his men were doing a magnificent job; we had no hold-ups due to a lack of serviceable machines. There were some Canberra strike squadrons based there, which seemed to operate at a very gentle pace. One day I came across a sergeant watching our men changing an engine out in the open. It turned out that formerly he was on No. 111 Squadron. He was standing there with tears in his eyes, and told me how much he missed the spirit and life on a fighter squadron. He was a former RAF apprentice, one of that group of men who formed the real backbone of the air force; John Griffiths was himself an ex-Halton apprentice.

Our squadron headquarters was a caravan over which flew the red and yellow chequers of our flag. 'Chiefy' Webb operated his orderly room from it in his usual cheerful and efficient manner. Each morning we would raise the squadron flag, normally accompanied by a rousing blast from Bob Roberts on a piece of gas pipe. How he could get a tune out of that weird instrument defeated me.

Our Adjutant was Flight Lieutenant John Vickery, who had a degree in philosophy and an Oxford Blue in athletics. He did not fly in the aerobatic team but did his share of normal operational flying and also acted as the team commentator and critic of our formation displays. Colin Hardie had done the same job on Treble One. Every practice flight over the airfield was filmed on 16 mm film, which was usually developed and ready for assessment within forty minutes. Our aircraft were being painted, two at a time, back in England and they were ferried out to us, usually by Wing Commander Browne and Harry Bucham. Harry was formerly on No. 92 Squadron and was currently a Transport Command pilot. He eventually became a captain with Cathay Pacific. Wing Commander Browne seemed much more relaxed when he flew out to Cyprus. The ferry pilots usually stayed for one or two nights and then took away two camouflaged Hunters to be painted. After some concentrated effort we finally had a good aerobatic team of nine aircraft and I flew fifty-three sorties in February 1961.

At weekends we relaxed. I recall cries of '*Shabash*' from Hamid as he hit the treble twenty with his dart and no one could ever forget the sight of Pete Taylor as he demonstrated his frenetic version of the Charleston. Later on whenever his name was mentioned, it was usually 'Pete Taylor, best Charlston dancer we ever had'. One day we managed to build a huge pyramid of beer cans in the mess bar. As the last can was eased into position against the ceiling, we all stood back to admire our handywork and a rash and rather brave young navigator from one of the Canberra squadrons ran across the room and dived into it. There was a tremendous noise as the mass of cans scattered around the bar. We were naturally rather cross about this, so he had to be debagged.

'You can't take his trousers off,' said Wing Commander Browne, 'there are ladies present.'

'That's all right sir, they're nurses,' said one of our pilots and we had our revenge.

We did three aerobatic displays during our Cyprus visit: one in front of the HQ at Episkopi, one at Akrotiri and one at Nicosia. The first one apparently looked quite dramatic, as we were able to disappear below the cliffs between maneouvres. On the last display it seems that we covered Archbishop Makarios in dust during a rather low pass.

In this period we had a small accident, the only formation collision we ever suffered, It was not serious in itself but unfortunately it was to have tragic consequences. On a practice flight, Frank Grimshaw, flying as number two, collected the downwash from my starboard wing. His port wing dropped and a drop-tank pylon collided with the top surface of the starboard wing of George Aylett, who was flying as number four. Frank's machine suffered no damage but George's pitot head was bent and he had no airspeed indication, so he landed in formation with me. The engineers decided that his starboard wing had better be changed and the aircraft was left behind when we went home. A few weeks later I had an angry phone call from the CO of No. 43 squadron. One of his pilots, who was carrying out the air test in Cyprus on our aircraft, following the mainplane change, ejected into the sea and was lost. There was something very strange about this accident as the pilot had given no reason over the radio for abandoning the machine and it turned out that he had ejected at least once before. Of course I was very sympathetic about his loss, but for the life of me I could not understand why their CO seemed to blame me personally.

On 9 March we set off for home via El Adem, Malta and Orange. At Malta we were obliged to land at the Fleet Air Arm base at Halfar, as there was a thunderstorm right over Luqa. While I was chatting to the Commander Air all my pilots vanished. I tracked them down in the camera-gun film section, where they were busy flirting with some attractive Wrens.

By 10 March we were back home at Middleton and we all had a week's leave. On the 27th we gave a display for the C-in-C, who pronounced himself well satisfied with our show – as he should have been, because by then our nine-ship display was at least as good as the Black Arrows. We all realized, however, that it was going to be very difficult to get out of their shadow. In order to look as good we were going to have to be better.

Our name was giving us problems. Someone decided we should be called the Falcons, but we did not like that much. Our problem was solved by a German journalist who referred to us as looking like *blau diamanten* in the sky. That was it and from then on we were the Blue Diamonds. (There is a coincidence here – Treble One got their name from a French journalist who called them *les flèches noir*, the Black Arrows.) Our aircraft looked magnificent. Each pilot had his name on the fuselage below the cockpit on the left side and on the right were the names of the fitter and rigger. Sometimes all three could be seen busy polishing the aircraft with wax. I also did my bit with the polishing rags; I think it did the ground crew good to see their officers doing a bit of honest work.

By now I was doing most of the leading in our two-seat Hunter Mk 7; this gave us an extra aircraft to play with and the longer nose did not really show at the front of the formation. I was also able to fly journalists and cameramen with me and because the Mk 7 had 3,000 lb less thrust than the Mk 6s, the latter could not be left behind.

In April 1961 the display season got started. We did two shows for Independent Television on 15 April and another at Wildenrath on 22 April. In May we were off to Norway and gave shows at Stavanger and Bergen. Following our participation in Exercise Matador, we performed at North Weald, Hucknall and Yeadon. The weather was very poor at Yeadon, which limited what we could do, but the press gave us a good write-up because many of the participants did not show up at all.

By now we had increased the team from nine aircraft to twelve and were able to use all the pilots by a system of rotation. Up to this point I had used the most experienced men on the shows, but Chan Biss told me some of the others were getting restless, so it was obviously time to get everyone involved. We then moved to our new permanent base at Leconfield, in Yorkshire, where we were made to feel most welcome by the station commander, Buck Courtney, and Eric Batchelor, the Wing Commander Flying. Leconfield was the home of Nos. 19 and 72, squadrons but 72 were in the process of disbanding – how often that depressing word was being used now as our fighter force melted away. One of their pilots was the New Zealander, Trevor Bland, whom I had known in the Far East where he was with No. 14 (F) Squadron, RNZAF, flying Venoms. He approached me at Leconfield and asked if there was any chance of joining No. 92. I telephoned the personnel officer at Fighter Command HQ and said that I would like to have him join us. I explained that although he had not flown Hunters he was an experienced Vampire, Venom and Javelin pilot. 'Taff' Freeman was a QF1 and could check him out in the Hunter in no time. It was all settled and Trevor, to his great delight, joined us. By 1962 we had three South Africans, a Rhodesian, a Pakistani, two New Zealanders, a chap born in Hong Kong, a Scot and a Welshman, as well as our English pilots. I believe this mixture of the Commonwealth was part of our strength.

We did several displays in May and June in the UK and Europe. A pleasant evening was spent in the officers' club at Bentwaters, home of the American 92nd Fighter Squadron, which was commanded by an impressive African-American, Colonel Chappie James, who later became a general.

On one occasion we had a delayed departure to Wiesbaden because of fog at the destination. When we arrived over Wiesbaden with our twelve aircraft it was well into dusk and the fog had rolled in again, so we had to divert to Wildenrath. This could have been an awkward moment for an average day fighter-squadron with only twenty-five minutes of fuel left. We were going to have to fly in close formation at night in cloud. 'Sections line astern, Go,'. 'Aircraft right-hand finger four, Go.'

CRDF bearings from Wildenrath tower were given, our navigation lights were all on and down we went through the strato cumulus cloud into the pitch darkness below. As we lined up with the main runway, 'Aircraft echelon starboard, go.' The aircraft broke downwind in turn and we came in for a stream landing in the dark – piece of cake! The station commander came out in his landrover and looked rather startled to see the long line of blue Hunters on his tarmac.

Naturally we went up to the officers' mess bar for a refreshing pint of good German beer. 'Hey boss, look at this,' said one of my pilots, producing a strange bottle which made what looked like a golden snowstorm when it was shaken. It was called Danziger Goldwasser and of course we had to sample it. The next morning, as we left for Wiesbaden, we wished we hadn't bothered. The weather was still not good so we flew in pairs at low level, turned right at the Rhine and thence to Wiesbaden.

We gave a display at Mönchengladbach in poor weather, operating from Wildenrath. The *Burgermeister* gave us a reception at the town hall, for which we were a little late arriving as our German bus driver got lost. The squadron got a wall plaque and each pilot a silk scarf from the *Burgermeister*.

Next we were off to Ahlhorn, home of the Richthofen Wing of the *Luftwaffe* – bad weather again. We had to let down over the North Sea with the aid of the Jever radar, then go back over Jever and down the railway line past Oldenburg to Ahlhorn at low level in quite heavy rain. We did what we could in the weather conditions. That evening we found ourselves in the company of Colonel Erich Hartmann and his German pilots, and Captain André Capion and the French aerobatic team. Hartmann is the most successful fighter pilot in history, credited with an incredible 352 aircraft destroyed, mostly Russian, but including five Mustangs in one day. He had been shot down or crashed at least ten times and had spent years in captivity in Russia following the war. A slight, fair-haired figure, he looked much younger than his years and was obviously revered by his pilots. He had the Knight's Cross with Oak Leaves, Swords and Diamonds, which was equivalent to having a DSO and three.

We were all in a room with a huge portrait of the Red Baron over the fireplace. Hartmann called to the waiters and everyone had their glasses filled with Schnapps. He then faced the portrait and called out, 'Gentlemen, Herr Baron.' All the German pilots repeated the toast, clicked their heels, and having knocked back their drinks, hurled the empty glasses into the fireplace. We naturally joined in, thinking it was all very amusing. André was not too happy, however, muttering under his breath about the 'bad mannered Boche'. I thought I had better defuse the situation and called for more drinks. Facing the French, I raised my glass and called, 'Gentlemen, Georges Guynemer.' There followed another barrage of breaking glass and then André, in turn, toasted Albert Ball or Mickey Mannock, or some other old Royal Flying Corps ace. By now things were becoming rather hazy; Hartmann had started the whole thing very much tongue in cheek. I ended the evening in the German NCO pilots' mess in his company, and he entertained everyone by singing rude RAF songs – I can't imagine where he had learned them.

To refute the myth that Germans have no sense of humour, here is a nice little story. NATO had a joint trials squadron evaluating the Harrier in its early days. One of the pilots was the German Second World War ace, Barkhorn. He crashed a Harrier, and as he walked back into the crew room, he said, 'Ah well, I'll catch up with that fellow Hartmann yet.'

So the summer went on, with displays at Exeter, Lulsgate, Turnhouse, Skegness, Bagington, Hullavington and Culdrose. Then we got a nice little job: we were to do a low flypast over London with sixteen aircraft on 19 July, when The Prime Minister was to inaugurate the Trenchard Memorial. We did a 'dry run' just as far as the lower Thames on 17 July. On the day itself we were told to delay forty-five seconds as we approached the Thames. Round we went through 360 degrees, using 60 degrees of bank. We turned right at the Thames flying at about 400 ft and headed straight for the Victoria Embankment Gardens. Harold MacMillan apparently stumbled slightly as he approached the statue carrying a wreath, which caused a delay of a second or so. I was told later that we passed overhead at the exact moment that he laid the wreath. Our luck was holding up and everyone was frightfully impressed.

I was now doing virtually all the leading in the two-seater Hunter 7, I believe that in the Yorkshire Air Museum there is now a Hunter 7 in Blue Diamonds livery. John Griffiths usually flew with me on the overseas deployments and the ground crew were flown in a Transport Command aircraft together with a collection of spares and tools. Group Captain Courtney and Wing Commander Batchelor also frequently flew with me in the two-seater.

It was now time for serious work on the sixteen-aircraft formation. On Treble One we had never got it quite right. The wing men were too far apart and the line-astern men too close, so the shape was wrong. We had to get the wing men closer and make the formation more compact. The aim was to get the sixteen formation as tight as the nine. With so many machines flying so close I was going to have to be very smooth, and numbers two, three and six (Chan Biss, 'Taff' Freeman and Bill Stoker) would have to be steady as a rock.

By late August we had got it right and we did a dress rehearsal for Farnborough over Church Fenton at the request of a group captain from the group HQ there. We were to operate out of the Hawker airfield at Dunsfold for Farnborough week, which was a pity as it meant that part of the show was lost to the crowd. During the shows a number of people flew in my aircraft with me: Bill Bedford's son Peter, Joe Blyth, Don Oakden's father, Pete Latham and, on one rather memorable day, Tony Bartley, who had been a distinguished pilot with No. 92 Squadron during the Battle of Britain.

On the day, 8 September, there was a very awkward cloud moving across our approach line. As I pulled up into a loop I realized we were going to enter it for a few seconds. This would normally be no problem, but this particular cloud was rather horrid. It had obviously sucked up a lot of dust and fine debris, probably from London, and for several seconds my pilots could see nothing except the white wing-tips of the adjacent aircraft. Pete Taylor, flying number sixteen, could see nothing at all, and he instinctively reduced the back pressure on his control column. The net result was that he popped out of the cloud a fraction of a second before the other fifteen appeared, which apparently caused a bit of a gasp from the crowd. Pete was back in position very quickly, so no real harm was done; I was of course unaware of any problem until the next wing-over, when Tony Aldridge called up and said, 'For Christ's sake boss, don't go into that cloud again.' When we landed back at Dunsfold, Pete Taylor was almost in tears, as he felt he had let the side down. Of course he had not; if there was any fault at all, it was mine. Still the boys were a bit shaken and several of them were grateful for a swig of vodka, a bottle of which Tony Bartley had in his car.

After the final show at Farnborough someone had organized a treat. Into Dunsfold came an Avro 748 flown by the Avro test pilot. This was to be our lift back to Farnborough for the President of the SBAC's cocktail party. As we climbed aboard we saw that every other seat contained a pretty girl holding a cold beer – what a splendid way to end the week!

Back at base there was time for a little more practice flying before the Battle of Britain shows at Gaydon, Biggin Hill and Waterbeach, which we did on 16 September. We also gave a demonstration for the Staff College at Stradishall and then got ready to attend an absolutely huge air show at Furstenfeldbruck, near Munich, on 23 September.

We had a new trick for this display. On our first loop we had four separate groups of four aircraft in box formation, which we joined together in a diamond of sixteen halfway through the loop. It worked rather well. The whole world seemed to be at this air show; I was told that the crowd numbered several hundred thousand people. We were the last team to fly and the immaculate drill by the ground crew, as all the ladders were removed in unison just before all sixteen engines started as one, went down very well with the crowd. I think on that day we gave just about the finest performance we had done so far.

Captain Pat Kramer, who had taken over the Skyblazers from Bill Creech, was flying with me in the Hunter 7. As we descended in the first loop, I noticed his white knuckles as he grabbed hold of the top of the instrument panel. I said nothing, but after we had landed he told me that if we had been that close to the ground in an F-100 we would have 'gone in like a tent peg'. After we had landed and switched off our engines, a German officer came up and asked us all to go to the VIP area. There we met the Defence Minister, Josef Strauss, whose opening words to me were, 'There is no doubt – the British are the best.' We had a brief, friendly conversation and then it was time to enjoy ourselves for a while.

The *Oktoberfest* had just started, so we went into town. What an incredible scene that is – huge tents full of happy Germans with their arms linked, swaying from side to side and singing away to an 'oompah' band. Chris Strong worried me for a while; he had one of those silly rubber hammers which make a squeaking noise when you strike something, and he was wandering around banging Germans on the head with it.

I need not have worried, because the Germans all thought it was terribly funny.

One incident is worth recounting. We had been 'adopted' by an attractive young Australian girl of Austrian descent who was on her way to visit relatives in Innsbruck. She had met one of the members of another aerobatic team in Greece and decided to meet up with him again in Munich. However, when she found out that he was married and had several children, she decided to change allegiance to the British. On our final evening we decided that a night drive to Innsbruck was not a practical proposition for her, so after a search of several cupboards, we found some bedding and made up a bed for her on the balcony which ran behind our rooms in the German officer's mess. The next morning I took her a cup of coffee and stood chatting as she sat up drinking her coffee, looking quite splendid in purple pyjamas. Suddenly a door right next to us opened, and to my horror out stepped General Kammhuber, the *Luftwaffe* Chief of Staff. The general's brief look of surprise was replaced by a beaming smile as he said, 'Good morning, isn't it a beautiful day.' He then re-entered his room. End of crisis.

I bumped into Colonel Hartmann at Furstenfeldbruck, but he looked a little preoccupied. I gathered he was there for a 'please explain' meeting with General Kammhuber. There had been an incident in the Berlin air corridor involving the Richthofen Wing, but then there were always incidents in the air corridor. I had also heard that Hartmann was now unpopular with the German Air Force hierarchy for complaining about the Lockheed F104 Starfighter that the Luftwaffe had ordered. He may have been correct; the F104 later became known in Germany as the 'widow maker'.

Back home on 28 September it seemed that the display season was over so we were back on normal fighter-squadron duties. Then came a surprise; our presence was requested at an air show in Tehran. it was decided that we would land at the Turkish air base at Dyarbakir to refuel between Cyprus and Iran. So on 12 October off we went again to Nicosia via Orange and Luqa, carrying the usual four 100 gal drop tanks. For this deployment we were taking just twelve aircraft, and we ended up staying in Cyprus for five days. Whilst there we gave three displays, once more at Akrotiri, Episkopi and Nicosia.

On 18 October we left Nicosia for Dyarbakir accompanied by a Canberra bomber as a navigational safeguard. Air Vice Marshal Worrel from HQ Near East Air Force was with me in the Hunter 7, and about ninety minutes after taking off, we had a problem. Dyarbakir would not answer me on the radio and the runway seemed to be blocked by trucks and earth-moving equipment. We had about fifteen minutes' worth of fuel left as we circled the field in formation. However, I saw that there was a long taxiway parallel to the runway; it was not very wide but certainly looked long enough so we sorted ourselves out into sections line astern, aircraft echelon starboard and carried out a stream landing. A bemused Turkish colonel joined us in the parking area and from then on all went well. But what on earth had gone wrong with the communications? Diplomatic clearance had been obtained and a flight plan submitted through the air traffic system. There is an old American military maxim that probably applied here. It states: 'In any military operation, at least 10 per cent of those involved never get the word.' The next leg to Tehran, flown over some spectacular mountain scenery, went well and we landed at Mehrebad Airport after a ninety-minute flight.

Our three day stay in Iran had its moments. Pat Kramer was there with the Skyblazers and André Capion with the French team of Mystère 4s. There was also a team of four F-86s of the Iranian air force led by the fair-haired Major Jabani, who had apparently been trained in Russia! We took off with twelve aircraft for our display and went into an orbit a few miles away as we waited for our turn. The French lined up on the runway and for some reason stayed there for ages. 'Come on André, get cracking,' I thought, as our fuel was disappearing at an alarming rate. Eventually they took off and we ran in for our display. We managed to complete the whole show but I told the team to lift up the four degrees of flap that we normally used and we completed the final looping break in the clean configuration to reduce drag and therefore use less fuel. One of our aircraft actually flamed out as the pilot reached the chocks, which was too close for comfort.

A Colonel Nakshavan had been detailed to look after us. We visited a nightclub one evening and had a couple of drinks as we watched the floor show. I had a bit of a shock when the bill arrived, but Colonel Nakshavan called over the head waiter, exchanged a few words and suddenly there was no charge. Obviously Iranian colonels had a lot of clout in those days. We also went to a splendid villa one evening. It was owned by the parents of a young man who had been at Oxford with John Vickery, and we had a very pleasant time with the cream of Iranian society. The daughter of an American general and her friend, a colonel's daughter, decided they would like to come out with us and the general sent along a young second lieutenant as chaperone. At the end of the evening the young American officer was in very poor shape and we and the girls had to lift him into their taxi. He may have ended up as a very senior second lieutenant!

All the aerobatic team leaders were dragged out of a party to appear on a talk show on Iranian television. I have absolutely no recollection of what was discussed but the boys said it was quite funny. I did not meet the Shah again but did meet the very pleasant General Khatami who was, I believe, the Shah's brother-in-law. He was killed in an air crash under suspicious circumstances some years later. He sent me a Christmas card three months after our meeting.

On 21 October we departed Tehran in three fours in loose line astern. During the climb, Brian St Clair called up to say he could not retract his wheels. Against my advice he decided to press on for a while to evaluate his fuel consumption with his gear extended. Under normal circumstances we had more than adequate fuel to reach Dyarbakir, but I was not surprised when he called me to say he was going to have to return to Tehran. Unfortunately he had left that decision a bit late and ended up jettisoning his four, empty drop tanks to reduce his drag before landing back at Mehrebad airport. His wing man naturally returned with him. So now we had a Hunter stuck in Tehran with not enough fuel capacity to fly out.

The landing and turn-around at Dyarbakir was straightforward, but on the leg to Nicosia my engine started to vibrate alarmingly so I reduced power and nursed it along, and the ten of us landed normally. Air Vice Marshal Worrell seemed unperturbed by all this drama. We had two aircraft stuck in Tehran and my machine had an unserviceable engine. John Griffiths, however, found a spare engine in No. 43 Squadron's hangar, so we 'borrowed' it and left ours behind. Our ground crew changed the engine overnight because we were due to fly to Athens the next morning to give a display there in two days. Then my ground crew warrant officer fell out of the door of a Hastings and injured himself. The problems were piling up and I wondered what else could go wrong. What else could go wrong? Then there was a ray of light: I ran into David Harcourt-Smith, who had just brought

No. 54 squadron into Nicosia. They had Hunter 9s and could carry two 230 gal drop tanks on their inboard pylons and two 100 gal tanks on the outboard pylons. I asked David if he fancied sending two of his Hunters over to Tehran and handing over four 100 gallon drop tanks to Brian St Clair. That was how Brian and his number two got out of Tehran.

We flew to Athens, where we were put up in a dreadful hotel. The display with nine aircraft went well and we all met Crown Prince Constantine, who was exceedingly pleasant. We had a small hiccup during the start-up when one of the aircraft had problems with a stuck fuel/air valve in the avpin starter. This was fixed in the normal way by pouring boiling water over the valve, although our normal precision was slightly marred by the appearance of an airman running across the tarmac bearing a steaming kettle of hot water. We landed at Luqa on 24 October, where I slept for fourteen hours. The next day at Orange I ran into Alan Jenkins and Billy Alcock from my No. 60 squadron days, who were ferrying out two Hunters for the Indian Air Force. By 28 October all twelve machines were back at Leconfield after another pair had been delayed in Malta by unserviceability.

That was the end of formation aerobatics for 1961 and, we thought, for ever as far as we were concerned. The aviation pundit Major Oliver Stewart had written an article in which he lauded our formation drill but said that we did not do a good aerobatic display. There are only so many manoeuvres that can be performed by a large formation. Basically there are loops, rolls, wing-overs, steep turns, bomb-bursts and formation changes. More exotic gyrations are not possible. We did everything the Black Arrows did, except for the one-off twenty-two aircraft loop, so what was Major Stewart on about? The real issue here was the nostalgia for the Black Arrows who had been first and were in the display business for longer than us and we simply could not get out of their shadow. That shadow persists to this day. There is a nice picture on a current website that shows sixteen Hunters looping in a split formation of four box fours. Only 92 Squadron did this but the caption reads 'The Black Arrows'. The same thing happens with magazine photographs. Any picture of a large formation of Hunters is assumed to be 111 Squadron.

As the year ended, I lost a whole group of our pilots, most of whom were to form the nucleus of No. 20 Squadron, which was re-forming in Singapore with Hunter 9s. Hamid returned to Pakistan. We were going to miss his phenomenal eyesight – he could see other aircraft in the sky at enormous ranges. Brian St Clair was to go to Warsaw as Assistant Air Attaché. I was awarded a bar to my AFC, to my surprise, and we all settled down to normal fighter squadron duties.

At about this time, the squadron had two interesting visitors. I had a phone call from London and the caller introduced himself as Professor Polk from the University of Chattanooga. He explained that his wife's brother had served as a volunteer with the Royal Flying Corps in the First World War, and that he had been on No. 92 squadron. His wife had expressed a wish to visit the squadron and he wondered if we could oblige them. Naturally I said we would be delighted to see them and a few days later this charming elderly American couple turned up. Mrs Polk was quite moved to see a photograph of her brother with a group of other pilots in front of an SE5 in our squadron scrap book, probably dating from

1918. Her brother had not survived the war. We entertained the couple at lunch in the mess and during the conversation I asked Professor Polk if he was by any chance a descendant of General Leonidas Polk of the Confederate Army. He said that indeed he was and expressed surprise that I should know of such matters. General Polk, who had been a bishop before the Civil War, had been killed by a direct hit from one of Sherman's cannon balls in 1864. Buck Courtney, the station commander, joined us for lunch and I think that the professor and his wife enjoyed their visit.

As 1962 dawned we were given a new and fascinating task. Every two years or so Allied Air Forces Central Europe held an air-to-air firing competition between the various NATO air forces. It was known as the Aircent Competition and the victors were awarded the Guynemer Trophy. The RAF had previously come second but the regular winners had been the Royal Canadian Air Force. They were obviously good shots, and they also had the ideal vehicle for this competition in the Canadair-built Sabre 6. This machine had the same power as our Hunter and was almost as good in all respects but in one area it was in fact superior. It had a fully-flying tailplane which was better than our electric follow-up tail and gave the Sabre better longitudinal response, particularly at high Mach numbers. Their 0.5 in Browning machine guns were far less destructive than our 30 mm Aden cannons, but the higher rate of fire, the higher muzzle velocity and the easier harmonization of their Brownings, gave them a huge advantage.

No. 92 Squadron formed the core of the gunnery team. We got some extra armament specialists from other units and from Germany came Flight Lieutenants Peter Highton and

Johnny Walker, the best shots from the squadrons over there. Also from Germany came Flight Lieutenant Mike Davis, an exceptional pilot attack instructor. The team was eventually finalized as myself (team captain), Tony Aldridge, Piet van Wyk from No. 19 squadron (he joined 92 full time later on), Peter Highton, and Johnny Walker as our reserve pilot. We then commenced a concentrated period of air firing at banner targets towed by a Meteor at 20,000 ft over the North Sea. The banner target was approximately 20 ft long by 3 ft 6 in deep and was kept vertical by a weighted metal bar at the front. We only used the two inboard cannons and loaded a total of 100 rounds of ball ammunition. These two guns were very close together and it should be noted that nose-mounted guns were much more effective than wing-mounted guns. For example, a pilot who could score ten per cent hits in a Meteor NF11, which had wing guns, had done well; but that same pilot should be able to score twenty per cent in a Meteor 8 which had its guns in the fuselage nose. The tip of each round was coloured with paint and each pilot had a designated colour to identify the strikes when the banner was dropped back on the airfield. The rules of the competition allowed each pair of fighters four minutes on target and only 2 attacks. The minimum angle-off on the target was to be fifteen degrees and the minimum range allowed was 200 yards. Any infringement meant that shoot was disqualified, which gave us a problem because the characteristics of our cannons meant that we had to fire down to just over the 200 yards minimum range.

At one side of our radar-ranging gunsight was a small amber light which could be programmed to come on at whatever range we wished. However, once committed to the attack, one's whole attention was devoted to the target and the gunsight pipper, and the little light always went unnoticed. Then someone came up with a good idea; the circuit for the light was rigged up to a buzzer which sounded in our headphones. This was much better; the buzzer was programmed to sound at just over the 300 yards range. Next we fitted some transistorized voltage regulators for the radar-ranging gunsight, which gave us a more stable voltage and better reliability. Frankly, all Hunters should have had them. Another small change we made was to the gun harmonization. From butt-firing tests it was discovered that a smaller bullet group was obtained by toeing out the port gun very slightly; possibly the gas envelope in front of the muzzles during firing had some effect on the trajectory of the shells. The armourers were working very hard and we got the stoppage rate down to an amazing one in 10,000 rounds. Mike Davis, in addition to analysing all our camera-gun films, was busy bore-sighting and harmonizing our guns and gunsights. He was also compiling a statistical study of which combination of aircraft and gun packs produced the best results. In addition to the gun firing, all the competitors had to do two camera-gun exercises in which they had continuously to track a target aircraft, which carried out a fixed weaving pattern. For four months we carried on with practice after practice and I calculate that we fired off about half a million rounds between the five of us. Finally, off we flew to Leeuwarden in Holland, where the competition was to be held.

The Canadians were brimming with confidence; one said to me, 'I'll bet you one thousand dollars we beat you.' I came across Wing Commander Joe Bodien, my old CO from No. 29 squadron who was now in the RCAF and he told me we did not have a prayer. They were so sure of themselves they had even left the Guynemer Trophy back in Ottawa. The name of their ace, Chuck Weingarten, was on all their lips.

At last I took off with Tony Aldridge on my wing for the first shoot. There was the Meteor tug at 20,000 ft and the airborne judge in another aircraft, well out of the way. We pulled into position high on the target's right hand side. 'Bentley One turning in now,' I said. The airborne judge hit his stopwatch; we had four minutes.

A dive down to the left, reverse into a right turn for the classic curve of pursuit approach, the gun trigger on 'live,' the slip ball in the middle, flying as smoothly as possible, the pipper on the middle of the flag target. 'Beep' went the headphones. I squeezed the trigger, the cannons rattled for about two seconds, I reversed left and climbed back into position for another attack. Tony did the same a few seconds behind me. We repeated the attack and our shoot was completed well within the four minute limit.

We landed back at Leeuwarden and walked over to the flag-marking area where two senior Italian officers were to mark the scores. The jeep arrived with our flag which was spread out: there were well over 100 holes in it! Tony and I had both scored more than 50 per cent. I noticed a couple of Canadian jaws drop; It must have been a sobering sight for any bomber crew in the audience as it would only take two or three hits by 30 mm cannon shells to shoot down an aircraft. So far so good, but it was not long before I was brought down to earth. The films were developed, and Mike Davis ran the projector with Major Graz of the *Luftwaffe*, our film judge looking on. My first attack looked beautiful. Firing commenced at about 300 yards and finished at around 220, and the minimum angle-off was more than 25 degrees. The second attack was the same. The cessation of vibration on the film showed that the guns stopped well above 200 yards. But it continued to click over: 210, 200, 190, 185, then it stopped. The camera had run on after I released the trigger; this had happened before. Or was that what had happened? Could I have kept the trigger pressed for a second after the cannons ran out of ammunition? I shall never know the answer, and in any case it did not matter. Despite the fact that I had obviously ceased firing at well over 200 yards, the last frame of my camera-gun film showed 185 yards and that meant that my 55 per cent score was now zero. I did not sleep very well that night.

The next task was the cine weave exercise, which went very well, thanks in no small measure to the accurate flying by the target aircraft flown by Tony Aldridge. Some years later I was told that this film of mine was used as a demonstration film at the Fighter Weapons School. So the competition proceeded; we all did eight shoots and two camera-gun exercises. The Canadians hurriedly had to send for the Guynemer Trophy just in case. We had one stoppage and I lost about twenty rounds on one shoot, which was hard luck on the armourers after all their good work. I cannot remember the exact scores but I know that Tony and I had another flag on which we both got more than 50 per cent hits, the highest-scoring flag of the competition. Pete Highton and Piet van Wyk were shooting well and at the end, after thirty-two firing sorties, we had averaged above 40 per cent. We had won. It was no fluke; we had achieved the highest average ever recorded. Of course the Canadians came a close second, the Belgians were third and the Dutch fourth. The Norwegians came last, but they had enjoyed themselves. It seemed that wherever one looked in Leeuwarden, there was a Norwegian airman in the company of a pretty Dutch girl, usually sharing a bicycle.

There was one more task at Leeuwarden: a parade to receive winners' medals from Prince Bernhardt. We formed up offset to one side of the VIP station and I scratched my head, wondering how to organize things. I put the officers in front of the ranks in review order. We set off, did a left incline followed by a right incline. As we approached Prince Bernhardt I remembered to shout 'Halt' as my right foot was passing my left. To my amazement there was one loud crash as everyone stopped together. At the party that evening, Air Chief Marshal the Earl of Bandon came up to me and said, 'Well done Brian; I see you have rewritten the bloody drill book.'

Everyone was very pleased back home and we had a party in the mess at Leconfield. We hardly had time to catch our breath, however, when we were needed for another task. Fighter Command HQ wanted to know if we could produce a sixteen-aircraft team for the 1962 Farnborough Show. This was a problem, as we only had about ten weeks and since the previous year we had lost Brian St Clair, 'Taff' Freeman, Dick Calvert, Hamid Anwar, George Aylett, 'Chips' Carpenter, Derek Gill and Jerry Seavers. We had gained Piet van Wyk, Tim Nelson and Dougie Bridson, who had plenty of experience on fighters but Dave Kuun from South Africa, Dick Ingham from New Zealand and Pete Carter were too inexperienced. I told Fighter Command that we would need some more experienced pilots. As a result Brian St Clair was attached back; he arrived literally jumping with joy. Paddy Hine and Alan Brindle then turned up. Paddy was due to take over No. 92 from me later in the year. These two were both former Black Arrows, so that was good. We had also got Hank Martin a little earlier.

I then considered what we could do that was different. At Munich at the end of the previous year we had commenced our display by looping four sections of four aircraft separated into what was virtually a diamond of diamonds. Halfway through the loop these four sections rejoined into a single unit of sixteen aircraft. My plan was to split up again into four teams of four aircraft for a co-ordinated display to finish off our show. The four sections would be Red, White, Blue and Green sections. (The pilots names and their positions in the team are shown at Appendix B). My four was Red Section and initially White would be on the right. Blue on my left and Green behind. The other section leaders were Frank Grimshaw, Tony Aldridge and Pete Taylor. Before the final split into four fours, we were to carry out several manoeuvres alternating with the nine Lightnings of No. 74 squadron led by Squadron Leader John Howe. Viewed from the centre of the crowd line, our show was planned as follows:

1. Dougie Bridson would come in from the left, very low and very fast and then pull up into a series of vertical rolls trailing smoke.
2. We would appear, offset about 30 degrees to the right, and pull up into a loop from low level in the split formation of a big diamond formed of four individual sections of four aircraft.

3. The four sections would then re-form into one big formation of sixteen halfway through the loop whilst inverted. This formation would then descend from the loop with the rear men trailing smoke and from the loop enter a tight right-hand turn, passing in front of the crowd from right to left.

4. Following a steep wing-over, the diamond of sixteen would then carry out a barrel roll, passing from left to right, the rear men again using smoke.

5. Next would come another loop with the formation changing halfway through the loop into the diamond 'T' formation with the front seven aircraft in line abreast, the rear men again trailing smoke. The formation would then change back into the diamond sixteen for another tight turn to the right.

6. Following another steep wing-over, we would come back in towards the centre of the crowd line for a double loop. As we descended from the first loop, White and Blue Sections would break away to right and left at 90 degrees, trailing smoke.

7. Red and Green Sections would then enter a second loop. Red Section would bomb-burst upwards at 90 degrees to each other when the formation was vertical, trailing smoke. Green Section would then bomb-burst downwards trailing smoke when their aircraft were pointing vertically down.

8. White and Blue Sections would then reappear from the crowds left and right respectively and each carry out a head-on barrel roll using smoke.

9. As Red Section position for their final manoeuvre, White Section perform a loop and a downward bomb-burst and Blue Section climb vertically through their smoke trail and bomb-burst upwards.

10. Red Section meanwhile would have flown outbound individually at 3,500 ft. At a call from me, each aircraft would then half roll and pull through and as each aircraft completed its half loop, smoke would be switched on and each aircraft head inbound at high speed, aiming to intersect with the others just to the left of the crowd line. I was the low man and the other three each aim to cross over the aircraft coming in from their left. (This is known as threading the needle. It requires steady nerves and the use of smoke is vital.)

11. All eighteen aircraft (including the airborne spares) would re-form out to the east and run in from the crowd's right in a huge echelon (it is quite difficult to make this look tidy). Over the airfield each section would loop out of the echelon at three-second intervals and at the end of their loops fan out as they joined the downwind leg for a stream landing.

That was the plan and we now had to see if it would work. The other three section leaders now had much more responsibility and would need a good sense of timing and position.

John Griffiths and his superb ground crew got cracking to get all the aircraft on top line, and we started to practise hard. For many of the sorties we had to fly half the formation, as other aircraft were being prepared and serviced. Engines were changed and 'lifed' items were replaced – many of them a bit early because for Farnborough we needed every machine we had. There were some weird looking formations over the skies of Yorkshire at this time as we flew with only a partial team. But finally we were ready. The aircraft were in first-class shape, morale was high and on 9 August we flew down to Coltishall in Norfolk to work up with No. 74 Squadron. The work-up went well. John Howe and I got on well together and there was a good spirit between the two squadrons. Both 92 and 74 Squadrons had a first rate record in the Second World War; there is some argument about which of them accounted for the most enemy.

On 30 August we deployed to Farnborough for the week's displays. This was much more convenient than in the previous year, when we had to operate from the Hawker airfield at Dunsfold. Our machines were parked close to the pilots' refreshment tent, which always put on a very good spread for lunch. Mind you, some of us were spoiled, one of my pilots was heard to remark, 'Oh, not smoked salmon again!' The fact that we were parked in full view of the crowd meant that they got the full benefit of the neat drill by the ground crew, who looked very smart in their white overalls. The cockpit ladders were all removed together and all the canopies closed together. The start-up was quite dramatic as eighteen avpin starters made their brief, loud whine before the engines fired up. This was all part of the show. The radio check-in was brief and crisp, and having lined up on the runway we then took off individually at one-second intervals. I have never been a fan of formation take-offs on a runway by more than three aircraft. I do not think the spectacle justifies the risk. In any case Bill Bedford the Hawker chief test pilot thought that individual take-offs made the crowd more aware of just how many aircraft we flew so close together.

The shows went well. The boys behaved themselves and did not overdo the beer in the test pilots' mess in the evenings. Eight hours' sleep was a very good thing to have before a formation aerobatic display. We had a very tense few minutes on one of the shows. Tony Aldridge who was Blue One and not replaceable by an airborne spare, got his nosewheel cocked at 90 degrees after take-off. The wheel was outside the doors, which were partially closed. The resulting noise and vibration made his participation risky. I expect the problem was caused by jet wash from a preceding aircraft. I was then mentally computing the enormous changes required in the display. An airborne spare would have to be pulled in and the four by four coordinated sequences would have to be cancelled. Timing is very tight during a Farnborough display. A thirty-second error would be considered unacceptable. Then Tony called up and said he would get permission to carry out a 'touch and go' landing at Odiham, which is just a few miles west of Farnborough. He got his permission, lowered the wheels, bounced his nosewheel straight and retracted the wheels again. Back on our radio frequency he called me to say all was well and he was rejoining. It was now getting very tight for time, as I was just starting the run-in from the north for the first manoeuvre. I told Tony where we were and asked him if he could rejoin in time. After a brief pause the answer came back, 'Yes.' I dispensed with the airborne spare and Tony came flashing in from the left rear, dive brake out as he decelerated into position. Blue Two, Three and Four closed up. 'Blue Section in,' came the call and about three seconds later; 'Diamonds looping now,' from me. It was a very close run thing – well done, Aldridge.

On one of our practice runs at Farnborough, I was not surprised when Group Captain Hannafin in my right-hand seat ducked down during the thread the needle manoeuvre, as Bill Stoker flashed over our canopy from head on. Our closing speed was over 1,000 mph.

Apart from Farnborough we did a few other displays in the latter part of 1962: one for a visit by the Duchess of Gloucester, one for a NATO meeting at Marham and another for the Imperial Defence College at Cottesmore. Two days were devoted to the press corps, another show was at Hornsea, and finally there were the Battle of Britain displays at Biggin Hill, Wyton and Finningly. For me that was the end of formation aerobatics; from now on it would be up to the Yellow Jacks and later the Red Arrows, led by two friends of mine, Lee Jones and Ray Hanna. Years later I was to check out Ray Hanna as a Boeing 707 captain with Cathay Pacific.

I missed the autumn air defence exercise because Buck Courtney sent me on leave; he thought I was a bit frazzled after a hard year. We did quite a lot of night flying that autumn in preparation for the re-equipment of the Squadron with Lightning Mk 2s and finally it was time to hand over to Paddy Hine. The pilots threw a small party in the mess and presented me with a very nice gift, a silver tray with the squadron crest in the middle and all their signatures etched into the metal. It now sits in my lounge in Western Australia. I was very sad to leave and wondered how I was going to settle down to a much slower pace of life – by now I was something of an 'adrenalin junkie'. Whatever came next was going to seem pretty tame after commanding No. 92; they were a very good squadron.

CHAPTER TEN

Military Twilight

The RAF next sent me to the Junior Command and Staff School at Bircham Newton. Nothing special happened there, but I think they enjoyed my lecture. We all had to give one and I chose to talk about the 1862 campaign in the Richmond area during the American Civil War. It was a comparison between the two commanders, George McClellan and Robert E. Lee, and how the strategic genius and moral courage of Lee produced a victory against tremendous odds. I have always had a soft spot for Lee's Army of Northern Virginia.

I next found myself at Fighter Command HQ at Bentley Priory. I was called 'Ops One', but I never really felt that I had a proper job. From the high days of the mid-fifties, Fighter Command had shrunk by more than 90 per cent, but there was no shortage of staff officers. However, there were a few highlights. I managed to wangle myself a Lightning Conversion Course. It was a great aircraft to fly; it actually had navigation aids and an auto pilot, which was a change. Previously we single-seat pilots had to rely on a map and the Mk 1 eyeball. We did have distance-measuring equipment but it was not very useful by itself. I only flew the Lightning fifteen times and never really learned to operate the radar and the fire control system, but it did seem that there was a lot for one man to do. It was strictly a one-role machine, an interceptor. We desperately needed a fast strike aircraft and preferably a multi-role machine. The Canberra had done a good job over the years but it was by now much too slow and vulnerable. The C-in-C one day asked John Howe and me, what we thought was needed. 'The Phantom,' we both said in chorus. (How nice it would have been to have the Hawker 1121.) So eventually we bought the F-4 Phantom from the Americans and a few squadrons became operational in the UK and Germany. It was a case of *déjà vu* from the days when we had to buy the F-86. Then we were waiting for the Hunter. Now, far over the horizon, was the Tornado.

Then something happened which was very sad and showed the extent of the decline in our defence capability. Bomber Command decided that they were too vulnerable in their present mode of operation (no surprise there). They decided they had better attack at low level and approach their targets under the radar cover. The C-in-C Bomber Command spoke to the C-in-C. Fighter Command and requested our co-operation in a low-level defence exercise. The plan was for the V force to attack the UK in the East Anglia and Lincolnshire area. We were not to use our Type 54 low-level defence radar as it was felt that the Russians did not have anything so effective. So SASO got onto the Group Captain Ops who got on to the Wing Commander Ops who in turn got on to me and there the buck stopped. I had to produce an operation order for the exercise. I enlisted the aid of a young navigator staff officer who had been on the same Bircham Newton course as me. Next I contacted the few fighter bases we had left to refresh them on the old 'rat and terrier' technique. At a meeting it was decided that we did not have enough fighters to mount an effective defence! I suggested that we collect a few Hunter 7s from the Lightning squadrons and base them at Coltishall. Then the question arose as to who should be in charge of this temporary flight. I naturally volunteered myself and as no one could think of a valid reason to say no, I got the job. It was now June 1964 and I had kept in reasonable flying practice and still held a valid Master Green Instrument Rating. So the exercise went ahead and my wing man once again was Tony Aldridge, who was still on No. 92 Squadron, flying Lightning Mk 2s.

I was told later that we actually intercepted at least 80 per cent of the bombers. Some of them were still painted white and you could see them from miles away. Bomber Command was not happy. They accused us of using the Type 54 radar but we had not. Bomber Command continued with their low-level flying and it was not long before the Valiant main spans started to crack under the strain of turbulence at high indicated air speeds. While on the subject of Bomber Command, it is a sobering fact that in World War Two they could lose more aircrew in one night than we lost in the whole of the Battle of Britain and they got scant recognition for their sacrifice.

I found myself one day at the Royal Naval College, Dartmouth, in the company of John Howe. There was a big get-together of all the Commonwealth defence chiefs and senior officers. John and I were manning the Fighter Command display, which showed how we could deploy a Lightning squadron from the UK to Singapore using in-flight refuelling. The fighters would only land once during this operation and that would be at Masirah in the Gulf area. We also had two continuous films running, one showing a target aircraft being destroyed by a Bloodhound ground-to-air missile and the other a successful strike by a Firestreak air-to-air missile. On the final evening we were approached by Prince Philip, Lord Mountbatten, the Earl of Bandon and sundry other very important persons. Whilst Prince Philip was watching the Bloodhound film, I said, with an effontery which amazes me today, 'You know, sir, it hasn't missed once all week.' There was a brief moment when the earth seemed to stand still; Lord Mountbatten looked thunderous but Prince Philip chuckled and the Earl of Bandon gave a loud laugh. I was not sent to the Tower; instead the Earl invited me for a drink at the VIP bar.

Another pleasant little job came my way at Bentley Priory. The Norwegians had requested a fly-past of Lightnings over Narvik to celebrate the twenty-fifth anniversary of the 1940 Battle of Narvik. Norway is a very long country and Narvik is an awfully long way north. While the feasibility of this flypast was being debated, I suggested that I fly up there and have a look. Again no one could think of a reason for saying no. I joined up with John Griffiths, who was by now on the staff at Bentley Priory and we went to Leconfield, climbed into my old Hunter 7 and set off for Aalborg in Denmark for our first stop. This was like old times, as we enjoyed aquavit and pickled herrings at a pleasant cafe down town. John was coming to check on the technical facilities for the Lightnings on their refuelling stops. We next flew up to Oerland, near Trondheim, and the following day up to Narvik. As we flew up Narvik Fjord, at low level, I was conscious of a strange phenomenon. The cliffs and mountains were so massive and the air so crystal clear that objects that were 50 miles away seemed only 10 miles away. We flew over the town at the head of the fjord, and although there was not a great deal of room for manoeuvre, there was in my opinion, enough. We landed at Bodo to refuel and then flew to Gardemoen, near Oslo, to refuel again. The plan was then to land at Aalborg and stay the night. When we arrived overhead, fog had rolled in and we diverted across the North Sea to Marham. Finally came a short night flight up to Leconfield. That had been a very long day.

I managed to get in one session of air firing as a staff officer, at the Fighter Weapons School courtesy of Squadron Leader Roy Watson. I scored 45 per cent, so obviously I had not lost my touch. Also, courtesy of George Black and Treble One, I was able to have a go at in-flight refuelling behind a Victor tanker. Fighter Command went down to only five squadrons of Lightnings and later No. 19 and No. 92 squadrons moved over to Germany. With the exception of No. 11 Squadron all the Lightnings were eventually replaced by Phantoms.

By 1965 I was finding the whole scene depressing and decided to make a clean break. I opted for retirement after sixteen years' commissioned service and got down to studying for the Airline Transport Pilot's Licence (ATPL), the aviation version of the maritime Master's Ticket. Following several months at the Aircrew and Officer Selection Centre, I found myself a civilian with an ATPL endorsed for the Chipmunk!

It was a big wrench to leave the Royal Air Force but I liked my flying and could see little in front of me in the service except a series of desks. I imagined myself at the age of forty-five or so in charge of works and bricks in Technical Training Command and it did not appeal. The RAF seemed stuffed with staff officers and administrators; this huge tail controlled an ever-shrinking 'sharp end'. The attitude amongst the administrative tail seemed to be, play it safe and keep their jobs. We should have had a British supersonic fighter years before we did, and work should have gone ahead on a supersonic two-seat strike aircraft in the 1950s. We had lost a lot of skilled people to the USA and the 'British disease' of strikes and union intransigence seemed to be getting worse. I wanted to escape.

CHAPTER ELEVEN

Civil Aviation

The year 1967 was not a bad time to look for a job in civil aviation. There were jobs available with BOAC, British Eagle, Qantas, Middle East Airlines, United Airlines and Air America.

I liked the idea of BOAC but they told me to expect to serve as a co-pilot for seventeen years! I did not fancy the Middle East, nor did I particularly want to fly for the CIA. The Far East appealed, and I had an interview in the City of London with Cathay Pacific Airways. They had no jobs right then, however, and I finally settled for British Eagle, who mentioned the chance of a BAC 1-11 command within a year or so. That turned out to be a pipe dream, and I had not been with Eagle long before I began to worry about their future.

Like most RAF fighter pilots, I had no experience of using VOR or ADF and I had only done two ILS approaches in my life. This meant some expensive training in a Beagle 206 before I could take the civilian Instrument Rating Test. I made it on my second attempt; the ADF let-down was not good enough on my first test. Following ground school at Heathrow and the technical exam on the BAC 1-11, I went off to Dublin for a few hours training on the Aer Lingus flight simulator. There I discovered that airlines put people up in much better hotels than the RAF did. I stayed at the Gresham Hotel in O'Connell Street, where they make the finest Irish coffee in the world.

Next came some general flying and circuits and landings on the real aircraft. I thought the aircraft was big, although some years later I would consider it tiny. The base training was done at Middleton St George of all places. One night I found myself in the right-hand seat of a BAC 1-11 at Heathrow, ready for push-back out of the parking bay for a night flight to Rome, frankly, I did not have a clue. However, the captain, a nice chap called George Foreman, let me fly and calmly talked me through it. For the next few months I flew BAC 1-11s on short-haul around Europe, which was the best way to learn the trade of airline flying. For the last few months of the year, I was with Swissair on a wet lease from British Eagle. Our aircraft was painted in Swissair colours and the cabin staff were all Swiss. We each had a free furnished apartment in the suburbs of Zurich and it was a very pleasant life. Although Swissair was a very Germanic airline in so many ways, they had an incredible selection of foreign pilots; one night in the operations block at Kloten Airport, I ran into David Smith, now a Swissair captain, whom I had last seen in Johannesburg in 1949. The cabin staff were efficient and many of the girls were very attractive. I became friendly with an Anglo-Indian pilot who had flown Spitfires in the Second World War with the then Royal Indian Air Force. He had the very English name of Geoff Carleton; his father had been the chief horse trainer at the Bangalore race track. Our friendship even survived the time I turned up at his flat at about eleven at night with a three-piece Paraguayan band!

The future was looking bleak for British Eagle. The aircrew were a particularly loyal bunch and had even offered the Chairman, Harold Bamberg, the use of their accrued provident fund to help him out but to no avail. They were going under. I was trying to get a job on DC8s with Swissair when a cable came from Cathay Pacific offering me a position as a First Officer to start in three weeks' time. On 1 January 1968, I was on my way back to the Far East.

Hollywood should have made a film about the early days of Cathay Pacific. It was started in 1946 by two pilots, an American and an Australian, who used to fly supplies to Chiang Kai Chek's forces during the Second World War. This hazardous operation over mountainous terrain was known as 'flying the hump' and they operated from India to Kunming. Their original DC3, called Betsy, now resides in a Hong Kong museum.

Cathay Pacific suffered the world's first aircraft hijack when a Catalina loaded with gold was seized between Hong Kong and Macau. One of the perpetrators shot the pilot and the aircraft crashed. In 1954 a Cathay DC4 was shot down off Hainan Island by Chinese communist fighters. The captain, Phil Blown, ditched in the South China Sea and there were several fatalities. The survivors were picked up by a USAF Grumman Albatross amphibian piloted by Captain Jack Woodyard, who did a magnificent job of rescue under hazardous conditions. The adventures of the Cathay crews operating in Burma in the late 1940s would fill a book. They flew DC3s and Avro Ansons and were frequently shot at. On one occasion they were forced at gunpoint to transport a group of Karen rebels. This early history is well covered by

Gavin Young in his book, *Beyond Lion Rock*. I heard many stories about the early days, some of which may be apocryphal. Were large sums of money and jewellery offered to the crews of the last few aircraft to leave Shanghai as the communists closed in on the city? Did a certain flight engineer really have to be assisted to his feet when he fell down because his pockets were stuffed with gold? Was there a secret drop-off point in a toilet cistern at Dum Dum Airport, Calcutta? Who knows? But the airline was highly respectable when I joined it in January 1968.

Butterrfield and Swire (later John Swire and Sons), had the controlling interest in the airline. When I joined they had only five aircraft; there should have been six, but a few weeks earlier, a Convair 880 taking off from Kai Tak lost a tyre tread from one of the two nosewheels. The wheels were on a common axle, and this caused the aircraft to swing gently off the runway. At any other airfield this would not have been too much of a problem, but the Kai Tak runway was on a long, thin spit of reclaimed land which jutted out into the harbour, pointing at the Lymun gap between Hong Kong Island and the mainland. The pilot could not keep quite straight, nor could he quite stop and the aircraft fell into the harbour. Unfortunately one passenger was lost. Later Cathay got four more Convair 880s, one from Taiwan, one from Venezuela and two from Japan Airlines. The two former Japanese aircraft were a revelation – they were beautifully maintained and their lateral controls needed only about one third of the effort of the others. Bob Smith, the Australian Chief Ground Instructor and former Chief Flight Engineer, was something of a mechanical genius. He constructed a Convair flight simulator out of the harbour wreck, with help from the Mitsubishi Company and an electronics engineer called Ian Bartlett.

The British Civil Aviation Authority test pilot, Dy Davis, came out to certify this simulator.

He was the author of the well-known book, *Handling the Big Jets*. In the course of his visit he did some flying on the aircraft, which he described as an intriguing mixture of the ancient and the modern. He also said that the Convair would make an excellent training machine for Concorde pilots. The Convair 880 featured in a book called *The World's Worst Aircraft*, but I think its inclusion was rather unfair. The big weakness was that it simply did not have the range or payload capacity to compete with the Boeing 707s or DC8s, but it was very strong and very well finished. It was also fast, although in the interests of fuel economy, we cruised at Boeing 707 speeds, Mach 0.8 to 0.82. However, during descent from altitude, we flew much faster than anyone else. It had more sweepback on the wings than the 707 or the DC8, and with the yaw damper switched off, it could dutch roll like a drunken sailor. A resident of Hong Kong once said to me, 'Why is it that the Cathay aircraft always seem to be flying faster than all the others?' The answer was simple: it's because they were. The British racing green colour scheme that we sported in those days was very appropriate.

Some of the technical systems on the Convair were more advanced than those of the Boeing 707. For example, I flew both types for over five years and on the 707 I had ten hydraulic failures; on the Convair I had none. The engines were the real problem. They were straight jets built by General Electric, virtually the same engines as those on the

Lockheed Starfighters, and they simply used too much fuel. We got a dramatic increase in engine life and reliability by using derated power for take-off, and we only used full power when we had to. This is common practice now in all airlines.

It has to be said that the Convair 880s made Cathay Pacific. They bought them for very little and they certainly earned their keep. When there was a typhoon and wet and very windy conditions prevailed at Kai Tak, we would continue to operate after all the other airlines had quit. One reason for this was that once a Convair 880 had landed and the spoilers were deployed, it then had all the aerodynamic properties of a brick toilet and was firmly rooted to the runway. A Boeing 707, on the other hand, still felt like a flying machine right down to about 60 knots and woe betide the pilot who neglected to hold in plenty of 'into wind' aileron during the landing roll in a crosswind. The upwind wing,would come up, the other wing would go down and an outboard engine pod would bang against the runway. One Asian airline captain managed to damage all four engine pods one windy morning at Kai Tak.

Cathay Pacific was an Anglo-Australian airline, together with a few New Zealanders. The flight engineers' department was pretty much an Australian iron ring but the Manager Flight Training, was a Somerset man with a strong West Country accent. His name was Laurie King and he could be grumpy. When I joined everyone was terrified of him; amongst the pilots he had a reputation of always having his hands and feet on the controls during training flights. All I can say is he never did it to me.

In my early days, Cathay Pacific was insistent on a very high degree of technical knowledge of their aircraft. Bob

Smith, one of the heroes of the Burma days, would drone on about X and Y relays in the brake anti-skid system or the exact functions of obscure valves in the airconditioning and pressurization system of the Convair. The ground school went on for weeks. One night just before the top of descent into Tokyo, I was asked by a training captain to recite from memory the whole of the electrical fire drill. This was ridiculous; this complex procedure took up about three pages in the flight manual and that sort of drill should never be done without the written checklist, otherwise you could miss something important.

For several years Cathay Pacific was the best airline in the world to work for: the pay was very good, income tax was a flat 15 per cent and the conditions of service were first rate. There was a generous accommodation allowance (there needed to be in Hong Kong), an excellent education allowance for children and a very liberal travel allowance for leave, which for the aircrew was eight weeks per year. We worked hard and there was no feeling of 'us and them' between the flight deck crews and the management in Swire House: we were all on the same side. Although the Hong Kong climate was rather hard to take between May and September, everyone had air-conditioned housing, offices and cars and there was more personal freedom in Hong Kong than anywhere on earth. Government was about administration, not politics. The lot of the Chinese population (and it must be remembered that most of them had come to the colony as refugees) had improved steadily over the years. The insanity of the Cultural Revolution had died away by 1968 and the Chinese were free to carry on their favourite activities: looking after their families and making money. Furthermore the economy seemed to grow at about 20 per cent per year. The dynamism and energy of Hong Kong was in sharp contrast to the lethargic atmosphere that prevailed in Britain and the speed at which a large building was constructed by Chinese workmen with their bamboo scaffolding was simply amazing.

For about five more years we continued flying our Convairs and I rose through the ranks to senior first officer, captain and training captain. Our favourite destination was Japan, particularly Tokyo. The airfield there was Haneda, right on the edge of the city. Some years later Narita, much further from town, came into use. The Japanese people were courteous and friendly with the sole exception of the taxi drivers in Tokyo, who all behaved like bad-tempered *kamikaze* pilots. The draught beer was excellent and the food top class. The first phrase a Cathay pilot or flight engineer learned was '*Roppongi dozo.*' That was to tell the taxi driver to go to the Roppongi area, where the action was. Roppongi and Akasaka were our two favourite areas in Tokyo. Who could ever forget Rudi's German Beer Hall, The Hippie Crazy A-Go-Go and its unusual proprietress, Dolores, or the Club Dracula, where the waiters all wore face masks of characters from horror movies? Captain Geoff Green (formerly of No. 208 Squadron), pinched the Wolf Man's face mask one night and put it on in the street. Unsurprisingly, no taxi would stop for him. There was another place called the Cave which let us have as much sake as we could drink for 1,000 yen. Sake leaves the brain crystal clear but destroys the limb co-ordination. A certain flight engineer left the Cave one snowy winter night and tried to vault a fence; he broke his ankle.

There are two flights on the Convair that I particularly remember. On one, I was up one early morning with Laurie King, who was doing my assessment for promotion to training captain. The wind was such that we had to use runway 13 for take-off and landings. The cloud base was very low, about 400 ft and the visibility around 1,500 yards. There was only one way to get in that morning and that was to do an ADF let-down using the radio beacon on Chung Chau Island and then fly visually up the western Harbour, across Stonecutters Island, then over the Western part of Kowloon towards the famous chequerboard hill. This hill was close to the threshold of the runway, offset to the left and had a large red and white chequerboard painted on it as a visual aid to pilots on the approach. One had to do a right turn at low altitude to line up with the runway and the passengers on the right-hand side of the aircraft got an exciting close-up view of rooftops and washing lines. On this particular morning there were just three of us on board. We crossed over Chung Chau at 3,000 ft, let down heading 225 degrees on instruments in cloud, reversed to the left after one minute and headed back towards Chung Chau and let down to 800 ft (the official minimum altitude for this procedure). I can still hear Laurie King's voice, with its Somerset accent: 'Right, lad, nail that back bearing now. Zero four one degrees. Start a slow descent.' We broke cloud at 400 ft. 'Right, now keep your eyes open for Green Island' [a pimple just off the western tip of Hong Kong Island]. There it is. Number one ADF up to Stonecutters and remember the radio masts on the right side of Stonecutters Island. There they are.' The approach flap was already down and the landing gear was selected down over

Stonecutters. 'Hold your heading; that building passing underneath is the Kowloon Magistracy. Heading zero six zero. Number two ADF up to Tathong for the go around. There's the chequerboard.' (I selected full flap and commenced a right turn). 'There's the runway threshold.'

We touched down and the flight engineer lifted the flaps to the take-off setting. Laurie ran the tailplane trim forward a little, I applied the power which the flight engineer adjusted and I rotated the aircraft on Laurie's call. That was a touch-and-go landing and away we climb back into cloud, heading 135 degrees until past the Tathong beacon, then turned right and flew west just south of Hong Kong Island. We repeated this whole procedure several times and some of the approaches and landings were done on three engines. The go-arounds, of course, are done on four. This is great fun in a four-engined airliner but quite hard work. As we headed to the terminal building for breakfast (and that always had to include corned beef hash with Laurie), about six airliners were in the stack over Chung Chau, waiting for the weather to improve!

By all normal standards Kai Tak was really unsuitable as a civilian airport, but it was the only one we had. There was high ground close to the runway in almost every direction, which meant very bad turbulence in windy conditions. Some pilots on other international airlines, who probably only landed there once or twice a year, were apprehensive about flying into Hong Kong, but for us in Cathay it was home, so we were much more relaxed about it. Nevertheless, in wet and windy conditions, it could be rather too exciting.

The other flight was on the day I caught the edge of Typhoon Rose, the worst typhoon during my time in Hong

Kong. Ours was the last aircraft into Kai Tak that day and sitting on the jump seat was a captain from American Airlines. There was no problem with cloud base or visibility and the rain was still fairly light, but the big problem was the wind. It was about 40 degrees off the runway and gusting to 60 knots. Air traffic told me that each time the wind gusted it also veered closer to the runway direction, so it seemed we were probably just within the crosswind limits.

As we flew up the Western Harbour, the wind sheer and the turbulence were indescribable. Passing the chequerboard in a right turn at about 400 ft, I was carrying an extra 30 knots of air speed and that disappeared in a flash. I actually had to apply full power for a couple of seconds as we bounced along towards the runway threshold. Through some miracle the touch-down was gentle and I still had quite a lot of power on. I banged the power levers closed, raised the spoilers and was just applying reverse thrust when I realized we were almost stopped. The landing run had been incredibly short. The next problem was that my left arm felt so tired I had to reach across my body with my right to operate the nose-wheel steering, which was on the left side of the cockpit. My first officer and flight engineer were rather quiet and the American captain at the back of the cockpit was white as a sheet. Civil aviation does have its moments!

I would never have attempted that landing in a 707. It was just viable, and then only just, in a Convair 880. After landing we repaired to the Aero Club for a stiff drink. It was not long before a drive home had become impossible in the weather conditions; by my second whisky the wind had reached 100 knots and was still increasing.

No account of Cathay Pacific in those days would be complete without tales of the Hong Kong Aero Club. It was the unofficial Cathay aircrew mess. Like the Windmill Theatre, it never closed. On one wall was a big picture window which faced the threshold of runway 13 and as aircraft engine noise approached, the gathering of aircrew in dark blue trousers and epauletted white shirts would fall silent for a moment and glance through the window. There would be a chorus of 'He's too high' or 'He's too low' or occasionally, 'Bloody hell, look at that!' Down this big window was a diagonal line, which was only visible to experienced Kai Tak pilots. It represented the ideal approach path for a touch-down on runway 13 and now and then some visiting airliner got it horribly wrong.

The Aero Club bar was a terrible trap. It was too easy to get carried away by the conversation, and time just flew by. Naturally a lot of the wives detested the place. Every Friday night the chief flight engineer would hold court, drink too many whiskies and sack all the engineers within earshot, but none of them took any notice. Occasionally arguments would erupt and mild fisticuffs occurred. Over one short period that became so prevalent that the club was unofficially known as Madison Square Gardens.

One story sums up the ambience of the Aero Club, and indeed of Hong Kong in general in the 1970s. One evening I had just flown in from Japan and the flight engineer and I went off to the club. The first officer declined to come with us in the interests of domestic tranquility. After a couple of hours of general socializing, a rather irate lady entered the bar carrying a cockatoo; it was my flight engineer's wife. 'I just knew you would be here,' she said. 'As far as I'm concerned you can stay and you can keep your bloody parrot with you.' Upon which she plonked the bird on her husband's shoulder and stormed out.

Operating on the principle of 'in for a penny, in for a pound', the engineer stayed put. Time passed and conversation continued, interrupted now and again by 'Squawk, I'm a naughty cockie from the bird.' Finally the flight engineer departed and drove away up Customs Pass Hill towards Clearwater Bay. At the top of the hill was a police barricade looking for illegal immigrants. A Chinese constable took one look at the engineer and called for the British inspector; the flight engineer was probably not looking too good at this stage – Apparently the cockatoo had done its business over his shirt.

'Have you been drinking, sir?' said the inspector.

Came the reply: 'You don't think I look like this when I'm sober.' (I cannot imagine him getting away with that today,) but the inspector just sent him on his way with a request to drive carefully.

Driving in Hong Kong was rather like being in a dodgem car at a fairground. Nudges and scrapes were commonplace but the serious accident rate did not seem too bad. I suffered two side-swipes during my time there but both were at low speed. One was by a taxi driver and the minor damage to my car was fixed for free by his cousin, who had a body shop; that was the Chinese way of doing things.

It was almost time to say farewell to the Convair; the airline started to re-equip with Boeing 707s and we bought twelve of them from North West Airlines. We had already expanded our routes beyond the Far East to Perth, Western Australia, now we expanded further, to Sydney, Melbourne and as far west as Bahrain.

For some years Cathay had operated twice daily into Saigon, which could be exciting. The activity at Tan Son Knut had to be seen to be believed. There were two parallel runways, and they were in use flat out all the time. The airfield was crowded with bombed-up Phantoms, helicopter gunships, military transports, etc. The activity was absolutely non-stop. Jeeps with 0.5 Brownings patrolled continuously. Most sobering was the occasional sight of stacks of aluminium coffins, piled up ready to be loaded onto military transports for the final journey back to the USA. Sometimes we had to stay high on the approach and finish with a steep approach angle because there was a battle going on close to the airfield. One day I took off from Saigon right behind a squadron of armed Phantoms and thirty minutes later landed at Phnom Penh in Cambodia. As we came to the end of our landing roll, I was told to clear the runway immediately as they had an aircraft coming in for an emergency landing. To my surprise it turned out to be a Mig 15! One of our captains, Brian Lewis, took off from Siam Riep in Cambodia just as the Khmer Rouge reached the airfield perimeter.

We had a dreadful occurrence in 1972. I was on leave in Antigua and one night I was chatting to an American lawyer in the bar of the Admirals Inn in English Harbour. I told him what I did and he said, 'Oh, Cathay Pacific. They have just had a bad accident.' This rather shook me and the next day, as I was on my way back to England, I asked the BA crew if they had any information. They thought the aircraft had been shot down over Vietnam. When I got back to London, I rang Swires in the City and they told me the names of the crew. The check/training captain was Neil Morrison, an extremely likeable Australian who had done some of my early route training. The captain under training was Lachlan McKenzie, who had joined Cathay with me. The first officer was 'Chas' Boyer, who had been on No. 111 squadron with me, and the flight engineer was Ken Hickey, another Australian. All four were good fellows and all were married.

Bernie Smith, our Operations Director, went to the crash site with some investigators from the UK and the Hong Kong Civil Aviation Department, which must have been a very harrowing experience. There had been more than eighty people on board and the site was in Viet Cong country. There were no survivors. Personally, I do not think Bernie Smith was ever quite the same person again after this crash. Slowly the picture began to clear; it was not a missile at all. The expert accident investigators were certain it was a bomb, and they were able to prove that it was in the hand baggage of a lady who turned out to be the mistress of a Thai police lieutenant. She was travelling with the lieutenant's daughter, and he had taken out some heavy life insurance on the victims. There were other factors too and the circumstantial evidence against this policeman was absolutely overwhelming.

He was found not guilty of murder by a Thai court; as far as we could judge the only reason for the verdict was that the court could not believe any Thai would deliberately kill his own daughter. There was a second trial and the whole rotten business went on for years. Insurance payment, if any was given, was obviously very much delayed. The suspect was found beaten to a pulp in a Bangkok alleyway; he recovered from that but later died a nasty death from cancer. There was no pity felt by anyone I knew.

I never really liked the Boeing 707 much as a flying machine but I respected it. It could carry a big payload a long way. The Pratt and Whitney JT3 fan engines were efficient and had a long life. Commercially it was streets ahead of the Convair but for a while I did miss flying the only four-engined fighter in the world, which was my pet phrase to describe the 880.

One of the characters in Cathay Pacific was Captain Barney Smith, and Australian who had flown Spitfires in North Africa during the Second world War. He had crashed into the sea following a confrontation with a German E-boat off the Tunisian coast. He was unconscious when the Germans pulled him from the water and he woke up in an Afrika Korps hospital. Bending over him was a German hospital orderly, and the first words he said were, 'G'Day, mate. How're you going?' It turned out that he had lived for years in Melbourne. Barney spent a couple of years as a prisoner, although he did escape once and had a few days of freedom before being recaptured.

During on of my final command check rides with him he greeted me in the flight dispatch office with the words, 'G'Day, wings.' Our Aussie flight engineer whispered, 'You'll be all right. He only says that to people he's going to pass.'

We had a day off in Singapore and I took Barney out to Tengah for a visit. Pete Latham was the station commander,

Eric Bennett was the wing commander flying, Chris Strong, who had been one of my flight commanders on No. 92 Squadron, commanded No. 20 Squadron with Hunters and another friend, Denis Caldwell, was the CO of No. 74 Squadron with Lightings. I had a short flight in a Hunter 7 with Chris and later Barney was shown around a Lightning. He was very impressed and surprised at how big it was compared to a Spitfire. One of the young No. 74 Squadron pilots suddenly said, 'Captain Smith, did you get any decorations in the war?' We all cringed a bit at this question, but Barney handled it well. 'Yes, mate' he said. 'I pranged two Spitfires and a Wirraway, so they gave me the Iron Cross.'

He once took-off from Taipei in a Convair 880 when the surfacewind strength was 85 knots. That must have been an interesting ride for the passengers.

Barney retured in the 1970s and made quite a name for himself as an artist.

Cathay Pacific was now expanding like mad. We were getting the Lockheed Tristar. It had extremely advanced avionics and auto-flight systems, but in some ways, it was another 880. It did not have enough range and was also rather expensive to maintain. Some pilots had reservations about the authority of its flight controls in turbulent weather. Subtle political pressure had been put on Cathay by the UK government to buy the Tristar with its Rolls-Royce engines, rather than the Douglas DC 10. For myself, I was happy doing a lot of early-morning base training and type conversion work on new pilots in the 707.

We got pilots from East African Airways and Bahama Airways and there began a steady trickle of men from RAAF

Mirage and RAF Lightning, Phantom and Harrier squadrons. Cathay Pacific was becoming more like the air force every day.

Sometimes the world of aviation seems very small. One is always running into old friends in distant corners of the globe, and coincidences abound. One dark stormy night I was doing a command check ride on Jules Brett, an extremely pleasant former RAF Canberra pilot. We were struck by lightning three times in the holding pattern over Osaka as we waited our turn for an ILS approach. We needed a beer or two after landing and in the course of our conversation it turned out that the brave lad who had demolished No. 92 Squadron's impressive pyramid of beer cans at Akrotiri all those years ago had been Jules's navigator.

I found myself promoted to Boeing 707 fleet manager, a job I held for two years. With hindsight, I think that period was my best time in the airline. We did all the initial training and type conversion on new pilots, and all the long-range flying to the Middle East and the east coast of Australia. In addition we were responsible for upgrading first officers to captains. The very senior people had gone up to the Tristar fleet, where the politicians dwelt – and there were plenty of those in Civil Aviation. I tried to run the 707 fleet as though it was a fighter squadron and it seemed to work. We had the occasional fleet party in the Bull and Bear, a well-known watering hole close to the Star Ferry terminal on Hong Kong Island. The manageress, normally considered a bit of a dragon, had a soft spot for us. I remember one night singing a duet with Roger Stuart, accompanied on the piano by Flight Engineer Robbie Robertson. Roger was one of our few

Americans and I believe the song was 'I'm a Yankee Doodle Dandy'. Another flight engineer joined in, playing the bagpipes – with somewhat mixed success.

Many of us had boats, and happy hours were spent on the water in the beautiful eastern part of the New Territories. My first boat was a 12 ft dinghy with a Seagull outboard, and my last vessel was a 49 ft, twin-diesel cruiser with two 120hp engines. That was a lucky boat because after several years' ownership, I was able to sell her to a German banker at a profit of 200,000 Hong Kong dollars !

For some years I lived in a small house in the eastern New Territories. It was on a hillside and commanded a fabulous view of large green hills, islands and the sea. It was built for me by the famous Mr Tse and his group of Chinese workmen, including Albert the plumber and the simple soul who acted as night watchman. He was nicknamed Chairman of the Board by my friend Simon Creasy and could often be seen leading a small herd of cows, dressed very smartly in a sports coat donated by some Cathay pilot. Many of us had houses built by Mr Tse. At the bottom of my hillside was a wooden jetty and a Hong Kong Marine Police post over which fluttered the Union Jack. I used to boast that I lived at the last outpost of the British Empire – and I probably did.

Then suddenly it was 1980 and I was off to Boeing in Seattle to do the 747 course prior to becoming the 747 fleet manager. What magnificent machines they are. We got them through the insistence of Stewart John, our Engineering Director. John Bremridge, the Chairman, kept saying that the 747 was too big; he wanted to buy Tristar 500s, which I think would have been a disaster for us. However, we bought new

747 200s, with Rolls-Royce engines and from that day Cathay Pacific never looked back. The two men most responsible for Cathay's success, were, in my opinion, Stuart John and Duncan Bluck, who took over from John Bremridge.

I enjoyed my course with Boeing, although their flight simulators were not very good. My instructor used to fly Air Force One for President Johnson. Boeing normally used Moses Lake for training but that airfield was covered in volcanic ash from the recently erupted Mount St Helens, so we went to the heart of cowboy country, Glasgow, Montana. It was an old Strategic Air Command base and had a long runway and an ILS. I flew the aircraft from Seattle to Glasgow under the supervision of my instructor and, on arrival, carried out my very first automatic landing. Most of my fellow course members got off the plane. I carried on with the base training for about an hour, and that was me finished.

That night Simon Creasy, Ted Butcher and I went into Glasgow. We had a meal in a restaurant, the usual splendid prime steak. The waitress was intrigued by us. She approached and said, 'Say, you guys talk kind of funny. Where you all from?'

'We're from Hong Kong,' I replied.

The waitress muttered an expletive and walked off. A little later she returned and said 'Come on now, where you guys really from?'

'We really are from Hong Kong', I said. To which the waitress replied 'Huh, well you don't look like Japs to me.'

After the meal the three of us went to a bar called Sue's Place. There we listened to Kenny Rogers on the juke box and drank Coors beer with Amaretto chasers. A group of

American matrons arrived in the bar straight from a PTA meeting or some such thing. They proceeded to try every drink in the bar, working from left to right, and ended up in worse shape than we did.

A few days later, back we flew over the North Pacific. It is a nice feeling to fly a brand new factory-fresh aeroplane. They are always spotlessly clean, everything works as it should and they all have that lovely new car smell. Altogether, I flew three brand new 747s from the factory to Hong Kong.

Meanwhile 'back at the ranch', a big battle had been raging over traffic rights between Hong Kong and London. We wanted some, but so did British Caledonian and Freddie Laker. Naturally, British Airways was bitterly opposing all of us. When Cathay Pacific was turned down, there was fury throughout Hong Kong. We in Cathay had expected some *quid pro quo* for our support of Rolls-Royce. The reasons put forward for the decision were ludicrous. Eventually justice prevailed and John Nott, the UK Minister for Trade, reversed the decision. We were on our way to London and Hong Kong had regained 'face'.

I grew more impressed with the Boeing 747 when I did my first flight to Bahrain and London. On take-off from Kai Tak, I had 417 people on board, including the crew, and 20 tonnes of cargo. What a remarkable machine. Late one night as I sat in the cockpit ready to depart Bahrain for Gatwick, the Duke of Edinburgh came on board, making it the third time we had met. His retinue took over the upper deck. Later on in the flight we ran into some nasty clear-air turbulence which woke up the prince, who joined us on the flight deck. The first officer was Kim Sharman (ex-Fleet Air Arm) and the engineer was 'Tubby' Grant, an Australian. We all had a jolly chat and then it was time for the serious part. The weather at Gatwick was bad, right on minimums, and I decided to do a dual auto pilot coupled approach. However approach control put paid to that by bringing us in at 90 degrees to the localizer beam and too close to the airfield. The autopilot could not cope with that so I had to revert to manual flying. Down we came, on localizer, on glideslope, windscreen wipers doing their thing and nothing but greyness through the windscreen. Prince Philip was sitting right behind me on the jumpseat looking down through his side window. Then Kim Sharman said, 'One Hundred feet to minimum'. There was nothing to see and a missed approach and diversion to Heathrow looked likely. Kim was just about to call 'Minimum Nil Sighting' when a voice from behind me said, 'I can see the ground'. (He of course was looking straight down). That delayed the 'minimum' call by about three seconds and as a result, the First Officer was instead able to call 'Visual, lights in sight'. Very, very soon after that call we landed. To this day I do not suppose that Prince Philip realizes that the only reason we were able to land was that, in all innocence, he interrupted normal flight-deck procedure and that, strictly speaking, our landing was illegal.

New 747s were now arriving regularly as Cathay went on growing, but in my opinion we never had quite enough crews. It is cheaper to pay some overtime than to train a couple of extra crews. I was either in my fleet manager's office, instructing in the flight simulator, flying the line or base training. Quite often Patrick from the rostering section would ask me to do a flight because we had literally run out of captains. A captain came into my office one morning and told me that he had returned form London the day before. He still felt tired, but he had just been put on standby and then told he had to operate back to London again that night. That was not on. We had now become a long-range airline operating east to west, but we were still working to the old rules. Tempers were beginning to fray. Some captains and first officers were falling out and requesting that they not be rostered to fly with such and such a person any more. This nonsense had to stop and I wrote to all the 747 crews, more or less telling them to act professionally and grow up. The real culprit of course was jet lag caused by the time changes involved in long-range east–west flying and insufficient time off between flights. Another worry was the increasing use of sleeping tablets among the crews; some of them were overdoing it.

We were now getting some 747s fitted with the RB211 D4 Rolls- Royce engines, which had more thrust and better specific fuel consumption, and the aircraft had a little more fuel in the wings. Also the maximum take-off weight was increased. Now non-stop flights to London and across the Pacific were possible.

It was Stuart John, the Engineering Director, who was pushing hard for the non-stop flights to London and for some political effort to open a route over China and central Russia to Europe (the most direct route). We commenced the non-stop London flights via the southern route over south-west China, Burma, India, the Gulf, Iran, Turkey and central Europe. It was a little tight for fuel but it was successful. British Airways later announced the commencement of their non-stop flights with a big fanfare but they were about four years behind us!

In May 1983 I took our first non-stop flight to Vancouver and Canadian Pacific Airways were not pleased. Their 747s had to refuel at Tokyo. It was a good flight. We took the Hong Kong Police Band and were met by the Canadian Minister for Tourism. To illustrate the effect of jet streams at high altitude, the flight to Vancouver took eleven hours and the return thirteen. It could feel a little lonely over the Pacific and we only had to check-in with air traffic control every forty-five minutes or so using our long range SSB high-frequency radio. It was reassuring to cross the Canadian coast only about 2 miles off track, because all the way over the Pacific we had to rely completely on our triple inertial navigation systems. It seems that as each year passes, flying involves less art and more science.

To those unacquainted with the Boeing 747, the following figures may be of interest. Our take-off weight out of Vancouver was 380 metric tonnes of which 164 were fuel. We had a viable payload and landed in Hong Kong with about 10 tonnes of fuel left. Of course that was twenty years ago, the Boeing 747-400 series does much better. It has even more power, better specific fuel consumption, and 'Star Wars' avionics; very long sector lengths of seventeen hours, are now viable. Flight Engineers have been dispensed with; they have gone the way of navigators and signallers. Boeing have even got rid of the one small defect in the 747 handling. The elevator control of the 747-400 is lighter which gives the pilot better balanced controls – when he bothers to hand-fly it!

People sometimes ask me which is my favourite aircraft. I have no hesitation in answering that I have two; the Hawker Hunter and the Boeing 747. Both of them are wonderful in the air and pussy cats to land.

Flight simulators played an important role in our lives; we were forever being checked and tested in them. The early ones were not very good; they were very unstable to 'fly', far more demanding than the real aircraft. Instructors and testers needed to maintain a sympathetic attitude towards the sweating fellows in the driving seats. A simulator could become an instrument of torture if a training detail was conducted by a bully. Strangely, the pilots who had most trouble were some of the older, more experienced ones, who tended to overcontrol. I think the reason for this was that they were subconsciously trying to get a feeling in the seat of their pants from a machine which was made up of computers and electronic switches. The secret was to treat it as a simulator and not a flying machine. Some of the best simulator 'drivers' I have come across were the technicians who had never flown a real aircraft in their lives. Over the years these machines slowly got better, with ever more sophisticated visual and motion systems. I have operated flight simulators in Hong Kong, London, Dublin, Frankfurt, Tokyo, Sydney, Seattle and Singapore, and the one that felt most akin to the real aircraft was the Japan Air Lines 747 simulator at Haneda Airport. It was also 100 per cent reliable.

As well as a steady influx of pilots and flight engineers from the RAF and RAAF, we also got quite a lot of men from the Fleet Air Arm. As a rule they were confident, good aviators, but one or two did display a somewhat cavalier attitude towards aircraft. One of them was told by a colleague one day that Cathay Pacific was not the Fleet Air Arm and that we had to get them all back.

When you are in charge of a 747 it is like having a flying village of people. Some passengers can get obnoxiously drunk. Sporting teams and Pop musicians are not the crews' favourite passengers in this regard. Passengers can have heart attacks, women can deliver babies, some poor souls can die on you and I have experienced most of these things. In some situations it was very handy to have a large Australian flight engineer with you because sometimes muscle was required. Of course the vast majority of passengers are normal, pleasant people and, thankfully, healthy.

Air traffic control in the Far East could sometimes be below an acceptable standard. I was once obliged to do an emergency descent due to a pressurization failure, a procedure regularly practised in the simulator. As we hurtled down at 40 degrees to the airway direction, with all the passengers' oxygen masks deployed, the air traffic controller kept insisting that we maintain our height. He did not seem to understand that if we did so, then we could end up with some dead passengers. On another occasion, trying to get into an airfield at night in bad weather in company with about six other aircraft, the role of ATC controller was shared between myself and a KLM captain in another aircraft. The ground controller had decided that the situation was just too difficult for him to handle and he had gone catatonic on us.

Apart from the first non-stop 747 flight to Vancouver, I also did two other inaugural flights on the Boeing 707. One was to Port Moresby in New Guinea and the other was to Shanghai.

The Port Moresby duty was not very pleasant as we spent a night flying down there and the following night flying back. The in-between day was spent trying to get some sleep and swimming in the hotel pool. We did not venture downtown as it was considered to be pretty unsafe. Our arrival on the first flight coincided with the beginning of the wet season and the weather was atrocious with thunderstorms and heavy rain. The airfield had no ILS and we had to do an approach using just VOR and DME. The help we received from air traffic control was virtually nil and I was later told that a controller had been sacked for being drunk on duty that day.

Between the southern end of Mindanao in the Philippines and landfall in north-west New Guinea, our Doppler navigation equipment was useless as the sea below always seemed to be dead calm and the Doppler went off line. There was a radio beacon on the New Guinea coast but that seldom worked, so for quite a while we relied on dead reckoning and our weather radar in its ground mapping mode for navigation. All I saw of New Guinea on the first flight was a rain-sodden runway and the hotel, as it was pitch dark when we took off that night. I only did one more Port Moresby flight and was surprised to see that it looked quite nice from the air as we came in just after dawn. However, Cathay Pacific did not continue with this service for long.

The inaugural flight to Shanghai was much more entertaining and before the flight I visited Shanghai with Captain Frank Seaton (formerly of No. 208 Squadron) and a nice young Chinese junior executive from Swire House, called Andy, who had relatives there. We went via Canton, courtesy of China Airlines; a fellow passenger was the boxer

Mohammed Ali. Between Canton and Shanghai I sat in the cockpit of the de Havilland Trident on a three-legged stool behind the centre consol! It seemed to me pretty extraordinary that they had a five-man crew in the cockpit. There were two pilots of captain rank up front and the aircraft handling was of a good standard. They also had a radio operator who seemed to be the only person to talk on the radio. There was a navigator whose sole duty was to tune in the navigation aids, and there was a flight engineer who simply sat and stared at his gauges. Another extraordinary thing was that although the airfield was on the edge of Shanghai, a huge, densely populated city, there were hardly any lights to be seen on the ground and the airfield itself was very short of illumination. After thanking the crew and receiving a boiled sweet and the gift of a pair of scissors from a stewardess, we deplaned and an hour or so later we were in the Peace Hotel on the famous Shanghai Bund.

The locals were very friendly and the hotel had an air of faded opulence about it. The next morning we went for a walk before our meeting with Mr Run, the local boss of the Chinese Civil Aviation Department. Before long, we had collected a huge entourage of Chinese people, mostly youngsters who seemed fascinated by us 'Gweilos' in our exotic clothes; in those days the entire population was clothed in the Mao boiler suits.

Later I began to suspect that the colour of their dress designated their importance.

It was now 22 December 1979, thirty years since the last Cathay Pacific aircraft had been to Shanghai. We met Mr. Run and his interpreter and the meeting was straightforward. It was maintained that Mr. Run did not understand English, but I had my doubts about that. He seemed a reasonable man with a rather ruddy complexion and reminded me of my Uncle Fred. His interpreter was a thin, bespectacled young man who seemed rather in awe of his boss.

We were invited to a famous restaurant for lunch. Food is a very important factor in Chinese culture and ranks in importance right up there with family, face and money. All the same, it required a certain amount of courage to tackle one of the courses, which appeared to consist of pickled sea slugs. After lunch many toasts were drunk, which also required courage as the tipple was *mau tai* – a Chinese spirit and an acquired taste. After some much needed fresh air, we visited the old French Club in what used to be the French concession area of Shanghai, where we had a meal and some games of snooker, which were regularly interrupted by friendly young Chinese waiters bearing trays of excellent beer.

That evening, we had a real treat and the biggest sign so far that China was beginning to open up. A stage was set up and on trooped a fairly large orchestra to give what was apparently their first public performance for many years. The average age of the musicians was about sixty and they launched into their repertoire which was the music of Glen Miller, Tommy Dorsey and Benny Goodman. A complete time warp back to my Second World War schooldays. What was more, they were pretty good.

On 16 January I flew the first Cathay aircraft into Shanghai since 1949, and there was Mr. Run to greet us. It was a dark, wet night and my last sight of him was the rear view of his jogging figure as he returned to the operations room clutching our small gift; a bottle of Royal Salute whisky which must have been a real treat after *mau tai*. When I submitted the flight plan for the return to Hong Kong, the procedure was very low-tech. A clerk went to a wall-mounted telephone and vigorously turned the handle before passing on our details. The procedure must have been much the same in the days of Claire Chennault and the Flying Tigers. The rate of China's progress in the last twenty-five years has been simply amazing.

There was plenty of humour in our lives. One day, a nice German ground engineer called Reinhart Walter was inspecting a Tristar engine with a device called a boroscope and as he peered into the lens he had his peaked cap turned backwards on his head. One of our aircrew walked quietly up behind him and called out, *Torpedo Los*! I thought that was very funny but I don't think Reinhart was terribly amused. The inside covers of the aircraft maintenance logs were covered in cartoons and witty comments, mostly from the Aussie flight engineers. One day someone overdid it and a particularly rude and tasteless comment was written. This led to a stern notice in the crew order book by our operations manager, Captain Alec Wales, an Australian who had been a Bomber Command Lancaster pilot in the Second World War. His notice went on at some length about defacing official company documents, etc. Alas, next to his signature someone, undoubtedly a fellow countryman, had written – 'Get stuffed Alec'.

The former BOAC/BA pilots were an interesting group. Most of them were very good indeed, a few were not and some others could be unbelievably pompous. The most notable members of the latter group used to be called North Atlantic Barons and Jack Symonds, ex BOAC, told the following story, which he swore was true. Back in the 1950s, a Boeing Stratocruiser on the London-Shannon-New York run took off from Shannon one day and at the top of the climb the captain removed his white gloves and announced to the First Officer that he was going to take his rest. He then put on striped pyjamas and retired to his bunk. Some time later the Loran long-range navigation aid packed up and there was complete cloud cover overhead so the navigator could not get an astro star shot. This situation prevailed for some hours as they droned slowly west over the Atlantic, relying on dead reckoning for navigation. Then at last there was a bit of a break in the cloud cover and the navigator leapt up with his sextant and stuck his head in the astro-dome to get a star fix. At this critical moment he felt someone tugging on his trousers. 'Bugger off' said the navigator angrily, to receive the reply, 'Come down here at once, this is the captain'. The frustrated navigator did so and the captain then said 'Mr. Navigator, how dare you wear green socks on my aeroplane?'

Another tale of British eccentricity was told to me by my friend, Mike Webster, (ex 264 Squadron) a former BA captain. He was in Karachi and at that time a First Officer on Britannias. They had just started their engines and were behind schedule. The BA Station Manager was standing to attention on the tarmac to see them off when suddenly the captain said 'Oh dear me, Engineer shut down one and two please'.

The mystified flight engineer did so and then the captain called for the purser and told him to open the front passenger door, get the aircraft steps replaced and tell the station manager to come to the cockpit. When the equally mystified station manager appeared, the captain said: 'Ah station manager, I notice that you are not wearing your uniform cap. Now we really must give the best impression we can to the passengers, so be a good chap and cut along to the office and get it. When you are properly dressed, we can depart'. Unbelievable, but true.

Another friend who was a VC10 captain, committed, one night, the mother of all faux pas when he used an obsolete expression. They had a technical snag and when it was fixed he made the following announcement to the passengers – in all innocence and with no malice intended. 'Ladies and Gentleman, I'm glad to tell you that we shall be on our way very shortly. The technical problem is solved; the engineers have found the nigger in the woodpile'. They were in Nairobi!

My last couple of years with Cathay were not the best ones. The airline was continuously expanding but as it got bigger, it did not get happier. The operations department was on the fourth floor of the headquarters building and at one end were the fleet offices, the flight engineers' department and the crew rostering section. At the other end of the corridor lived the operations director and his staff and in among the staff were some people who did not seem to understand that loyalty has to go both ways – down through the ranks as well as up. Some bad decisions had been made and an unhealthy atmosphere prevailed. As Cathay Pacific got bigger the old 'family feeling' disappeared and I suppose this was inevitable as a result of their enormous expansion, but it was a great disappointment for me to read about all the industrial disputes they had in the 1990s. It would seem that in my era we had the best years.

I was just coming up to 55 and it was time to leave. My wife, who had not been well for some time had already returned to Australia and our daughters were at school there. I needed a rest and, frankly, dodging thunderstorms over the Burma-India border at 2a.m., had lost its charm. I had been flying for an awfully long time and considered that I was lucky to have come out of it unscathed as so many of the young men who had started with me had not. On reflection, the best of all times was the period when I commanded No. 92 Squadron. When it came to weapons scores, serviceability rates and the number of sorties flown, we were without peer and I owe a great deal to the pilots and John Griffiths' ground crew; without them none of it would have been possible. We were awarded the Dacre Trophy in 1962 which is given to the best unit of No. 11 Group of Fighter Command and neither before that time, nor since, have so many jet fighters flown formation aerobatics so close together. We were able to develop and expand on the principles demonstrated by Roger Topp, Pete Latham and Treble One.

The Red Arrows have done a superb job over the years using a team of up to nine aircraft, which is a nice flexible number and allows a good variety of formations. To use sixteen aircraft would be prohibitively expensive today. The likes of the Black Arrows and The Blue Diamonds will not be seen again.

CHAPTER TWELVE

Fini

By May 1984 I had retired in my new home in Western Australia – a very nice place to live. I had also bought an apartment on the coast of Granada Province in Southern Spain and we spent some holiday time there. Every year I also visited England and while there, I never missed spending time at the RAF Club on Piccadilly, where I usually met some old pals.

By 1990 I was feeling restless again and felt that gardening, golf and reading were not enough. Until 1987 I had done some flying in various Cessnas, a Chipmunk, a Tiger Moth and even a Harvard, far away in Texas. Then one day in 1990, I ran across Brian Floyd, who had left Cathay Pacific shortly after me. He also had itchy feet and had just joined Air Hong Kong, a small cargo airline with two Boeing 707-320 freighters. I pondered for a while and then decided to go and see them. They seemed keen to have me and I decided to do some serious flying again. I was sixty and so could not fly as a Captain any longer and furthermore I had to resit the technical exam on the Boeing 707, as I had not flown one for over ten years. From a 747 Fleet Manager to a 707 co-pilot was a big drop but I found that I enjoyed it and only now and then did I find myself saying things like, 'Might I suggest' or 'Are you sure you want to do that?'

Air Hong Kong had one good 707 and one terrible one. The bad one had started life with Pan American and later went to Egyptian Airlines. On every take-off as it lifted off the runway, it would lurch sideways, so at some time in its past life it must have suffered a real thump; the thing was bent. However flying freighters is quite pleasant in most circumstances, because freight never complains. The drawbacks are that most of the flying seems to be at night and one is always at maximum take-off and landing weight. This can give one the feeling that all the runways are a bit short. A wise American friend once said to me 'The best aide to flight safety that I know is the concrete mixer'.

I experienced some new places like Mauritius, Katmandu, Istanbul, Athens, Brussels, Manchester and Constanta in Rumania. Our main route was to Manchester via the Gulf and Brussels and during the first Gulf War we switched from a Bahrain stopover to Dubai, which we all preferred. The 707s were sold and in 1991 we got two 747-100 freighters together with more ex-Cathay personnel and some ex-BA aircrew. These 747s were a let-down after the brand new Rolls-Royce-engined 200 series that I had flown before. The power levers seemed to be connected to the Pratt and Whitney engines by bungee cords and I missed the crisp response of the Rolls Royce triple spool engines.

I went across to San Bernardino in California with Hugh Dibley and Jim Goatham to collect a third 747-100. They were both ex BA and Jim had been a Concorde flight engineer. I flew the first leg to Honolulu and found the aircraft to be pretty weird. The controls felt like no other 747 I had ever flown and the air conditioning was stuck on cold. On the second leg to Hong Kong in this flying refrigerator, we had to shut down an engine when it ran out of oil pressure. This machine was not a success and its cargo door gave endless trouble.

After three pleasant years with Air Hong Kong, I ran into trouble on a six monthly medical. One of my ECG lines had a funny squiggle and it turned out that my right coronary artery was partly blocked. After the cardiologist's report, which concluded that I had a $1^1/_2$ per cent chance of a heart attack, my pilot's licence was revoked. Doctor Doom was unreceptive when I pointed out that a $98^1/_2$ per cent chance of not having a heart attack seemed pretty good to me. Twelve years later, I am still in the ninety eight and a half per cent. I stayed on for a while doing some flight simulator work and looking after training records and then, in April 1994, retired for the second time.

It was back to the gardening and reading for a while, then one day Mike Webster telephoned me and asked if I was interested in doing some 747 simulator instructing in England for a few months. Naturally I said that I was and so for a few months in 1996 I was back in the world of aviation teaching young, French air force pilots to operate the Boeing 747 – and a jolly good bunch they were too. Just for a change one day, Mike gave me an Arab airline crew for a refresher training detail. About halfway through the detail I told them I was going to fail an engine on take-off during their next practice departure from runway 27 left at Heathrow. So, on take-off I failed number four engine (outside right) just before V1 (the stop/go decision speed). The captain not only decided to keep going, he also booted in the wrong rudder. Theoretically, we ended up in the Penta Hotel on the edge of the A4. I then uttered almost my final words in the world of aviation:

'Captain, I think we had better try that one again'.

APPENDIX A

List of Formation Aerobatic Displays Flown

13.2.56	Singapore	9.5.59	Wethersfield
16.2.56	Bangkok	10.5.59	Wiesbaden
27.10.56	Saigon	13.5.59	Wattisham
27.10.56	Saigon	13.5.59	Cottesmore
9.5.58	Spangdalem	16.5.59	Bentwaters
17.5.58	Bentwaters	16.5.59	Sculthorpe
17.5.58	Alconbury	18.5.59	Hucknall
18.5.58	Bitburg	18.5.59	Yeadon
11.6.58	Bitburg	18.5.59	Church Fenton
21.6.58	Rennes	24.5.59	Oslo
29.6.58	Liege	30.5.59	Shoreham
1.7.58	Odiham	6.6.59	Skegness
5.7.58	Soesterberg	10.6.59	Lisbon
10.7.58	Wyton	13.6.59	Chivenor
12.7.58	Bagington	16.6.59	Coltishall
23.8.58	Wethersfield	20.6.59	Paris
1.9.58	Farnborough	21.6.59	Paris
2.9.58	Farnborough	6.7.59	Waterbeach
4.9.58	Farnborough	11.7.59	Bagington
5.9.58	Farnborough	19.7.59	Tours
6.9.58	Farnborough	20.7.59	Bawdsey
7.9.58	Farnborough	21.7.59	Marham
11.9.58	Wattisham	26.7.59	Manston
11.9.58	Wattisham	26.7.59	Calais
14.9.58	Bordeaux	5.8.59	Sylt
20.9.58	Biggin Hill	9.8.59	Royan
20.9.58	Wattisham	29.8.59	Gaydon
20.9.58	Honnington	29.8.59	Abingdon
27.9.58	Odiham	29.8.59	Wolverhampton
4.3.59	Wyton	7.9.59	Farnborough
11.4.59	Bitburg	8.9.59	Farnborough

9.9.59	Farnborough	15.7.61	Bagington
10.9.59	Farnborough	15.7.61	Hullavington
11.9.59	Farnborough	15.7.61	Culdrose
12.9.59	Farnborough	19.7.61	Whitehall – London
13.9.59	Farnborough		(Fly Past)
19.9.59	Gaydon	29.8.61	Church Fenton
19.9.59	Cottesmore	5.9.61	Famborough
19.9.59	Felixstowe	6.9.61	Famborough
19.9.59	Wattisham	7.9.61	Famborough
18.4.60	Goodwood	8.9.61	Famborough
5.9.60	Farnborough	9.9.61	Famborough
7.9.60	Farnborough	10.9.61	Famborough
8.9.60	Farnborough	16.9.61	Gaydon
9.9.60	Farnborough	16.9.61	Biggin Hill
21.12.60	Ouston	16.9.61	Waterbeach
20.2.61	Episkopi	19.9.61	Stradishall
28.2.61	Akrotiri	24.9.61	Furstenfeldbruck
2.3.61	Nicosia	14.10.61	Akrotiri
27.3.61	Middleton – St. George	16.10.61	Nicosia
15.4.61	Middleton - St. George	17.10.61	Episkopi
15.4.61	Middleton-St George	20.10.61	Tehran
22.4.61	Wildenrath	23.10.61	Athens
7.5.61	Stavanger	5.7.62	Middleton – St.
7.5.61	Bergen		George
22.5.61	Waddington	6.7.62	Marham
22.5.61	North Weald	12.7.62	Cottesmore
22.5.61	Hucknall	6.8.62	Hornsea
22.5.61	Yeadon	20.8.62	Coltishal!
7.6.61	Ouston	20.8.62	Coltishall
8.6.61	Ouston	20.8.62	Coltishall
11.6.61	Wiesbaden	28.8.62	Coltishall
12.6.61	Coltishall	3.9.62	Farnborough
17.6.61	Wethersfield	4.9.62	Farnborough
17.6.61	Bentwaters	5.9.62	Farnborough
18.6.61	Mönchen Gladbach	6.9.62	Farnborough
18.6.61	Ahlhorn	7.9.62	Farnborough
24.6.61	Lullsgate	8.9.62	Farnborough
24.6.61	Exeter	9.9.62	Farnborough
1.7.61	Turnhouse	15.9.62	Biggin Hill
4.7.61	Skegness	15.9.62	Wyton
6.7.61	Cottesmore	15.9.62	Finningley

1962 Farnborough Team

The Blue Diamonds of No. 92 Squadron

Red Section
Brian Mercer
Chan. Biss
Don Oakden
Bill Stoker

Blue Section
Tony Aldridge
Paddy Hine
Chris Strong
Brian St. Clair

White Section
Frank Grimshaw
Brian Alchin
Alan Brindle
Tim Nelson

Green Section
Pete Taylor
Piet Van Wyk
Crawford Cameron
Trevor Bland

Spare 1   Doug Bridson
Spare 2   Hank Martin

APPENDIX C

Hong Kong and Kai Tak Airport

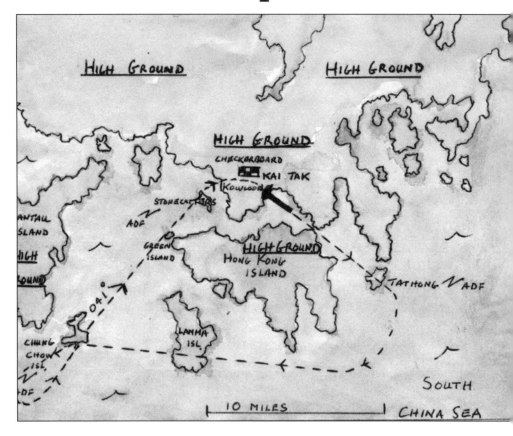

Route on training detail for Chung Chow A.D.F. Let-down and touch and go landings on runway 13.

I.L.S. only on runway 31.

Note that Kai Tak Airport was almost completely surrounded by high ground, up to over 3,000ft.

Index